HOW TO RESTORE
Electrical & Ignition Systems

CONTENTS

Introduction

Too many people have made the restoration of a car sound impossibly difficult, or expensive. Perhaps this was done unintentionally or perhaps there were vested interests at work. In particular, the study of electrical systems has sometimes been presented as a 'black art'. This book, I hope, will prove them wrong.

I have completed many repair and restoration jobs over the years, and I reckon that any competent 'shade tree' mechanic, with the right tools and equipment, can tackle the rebuilding of almost any electrical component of the 'pre-electronic' era. Clearly, now that cars are being fitted with on-board computers, electronic sensing in fuel injection systems, and other components sealed into little black boxes, scope for cheap restoration has been reduced, but I am still sure that we will be able to repair many of the 1970s and 1980s cars at the end of this century.

In this book, my aim has not been to encourage you to rush out and pay through the nose for an expensive new (or exchange) part, but to show you how small and often inexpensive parts can be renewed to give the same effect. In all cases I have assumed that you, as the enthusiast/ rebuilder, are conversant with the basics of a car's electrical system, and that you have a simply equipped workshop or garage to make the restoration feasible.

Your watchword in tackling electrical repairs and restoration should primarily be 'caution', but another should certainly be 'persistence'. In so many ways, the repair of a component will depend on your ability to locate, identify, and purchase the small parts required and *that* might be more time-consuming than doing the job itself. But, please keep at it. Your reward will not only be financial, but it will also ensure that you keep the vehicle's originality as well, and for a 'classic' car or 'collector' enthusiast that is very important.

Finally, as with most aspects of restoring a car, I would emphasise that you should plan the job, and work out a logical sequence of work, even before you reach for the socket wrench or the screwdriver. It will save hours of frustration, and probably a great deal of money, in the end.

Chapter 1 | A few words before we begin

The electrical system is the Achilles heel of all older cars, and probably the most neglected. People who will quite happily strip down and repair an engine or gearbox, approach electrical repairs with apprehension mainly, I suspect, because with electrical components you seldom see anything happening. A system which is completely dead, looks much the same as one which will work perfectly.

Once you understand the basic principles, and they are not hard to grasp, all the mystery disappears. My aim in this book is to show you how, in a simple and logical way, you can tackle anything from a burnt-out bulb to a complete rewire with confidence. It is necessary to know a little about electrical theory, but not much, so I shall keep theory to a minimum and practicality to a maximum.

The whole key to understanding electrics is to keep in mind the requirements of a simple circuit. I want to stress this, even at the risk of over-simplifying things. Think of electricity as going round in a circle, which is why its path is called a circuit. The four essential elements are a feed, a switch, a component and a return. Sometimes they run in that order, and sometimes the order is feed, component, switch and return. It doesn't matter which, but it's important to find out so that you know which cables are still live when you switch off.

Some older cars, and some commerical vehicles, have double-pole wiring, which is a system where the body or chassis is completely isolated from the electrical system and the return is by a cable. The vast majority of cars, however, have single-pole wiring where the metal body or chassis is used as the return, and usually referred to as 'earth' or 'ground'. The supply box for the system, the battery, has one of its terminals connected to earth. The other feeds the various circuits. After the electricity has done its job—perhaps of lighting a lamp or working a motor—it returns to the battery through the chassis. Theorists will probably throw up their hands in horror at this explanation, but it's the easiest and simplest way I know of picturing it. If you keep it in mind you won't go far wrong.

You might find either the positive or the negative side of the battery connected to earth. At one time all cars were negative (−) earth, then for various reasons manufacturers went over to connecting the positive (+) side of the battery to earth. Then when alternators came in they swung back again to negative earth. For practical purposes the system works just as well no matter which side of the battery is connected to earth, but you have to keep it in mind when you buy certain components and accessories, and when you are using measuring instruments. If in doubt whether or not a component is suitable for your system, *always* ask.

With regard to the tools you will need to overhaul the electrics, they are surprisingly few, so you can afford to

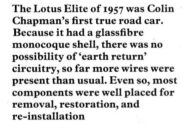

The Lotus Elite of 1957 was Colin Chapman's first true road car. Because it had a glassfibre monocoque shell, there was no possibility of 'earth return' circuitry, so far more wires were present than usual. Even so, most components were well placed for removal, restoration, and re-installation

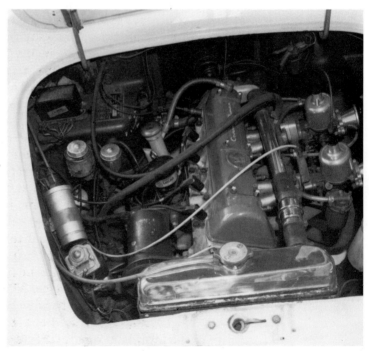

buy the best quality items. You will need a few spanners and a screwdriver or two, mainly for taking components off and for stripping them down, and a couple of pairs of good quality pliers, one with a normal square nose and the other with a long pointed nose. For stripping insulation off cables get yourself a proper insulation stripper. Messing about with a pocket-knife against your thumb leads to broken wire strands and trouble, not to mention a cut thumb.

I don't very much care for the cheap type of insulation stripper sometimes built into the handle of some so-called electrician's screwdrivers, the sort that's a metal plate with a tapering keyhole in it. A much better tool is the type of stripper used by telephone engineers. This looks like a small pair of pincers with two vee cuts in the jaws, and there's a screw at the side to adjust the tool for the thickness of the cable. Even better in my opinion is the 'Rolls-Royce' of insulation strippers, a toggle-action tool with slots for various sizes of cable, cut in a steel jaw plate. You put the end of the cable in, squeeze the handles, and you get a perfect job every time.

When you're working on the car, your fingers are bound to get oily, and if you twist the strands of stripped cable with oily fingers it makes them difficult to solder. A tip which avoids this trouble is to pull the short piece of insulation part of the way off and then twist it so that the wire strands twist together without your having to touch them with your greasy fingers.

You will need various thicknesses or 'weights' of cable for a car's wiring, depending on the current the cable has to carry. Cable sizes used to be expressed in Imperial units, but all the new cable you buy will be in metric units, so you'll need to understand both systems.

In both systems the cables are coded by a series of numbers divided by a stroke. It tells you the number of strands and the wire size. In the metric system for example, a cable with the code 14/0.30 will have 14 strands, each one 0.30 mm diameter. The older Imperial equivalent of the metric 14/0.30 would be 14/012, which denotes 14 strands, each one 0.012 in. diameter. Auto electricians often make a distinction between the two systems by the

Bird's eye view of the 1950s Lotus Elite engine bay, showing the dynamo, wiper motor, coil, and distributor installation. Note the extra strong fixings for the dynamo to the block of the Coventry-Climax engine and the side-mounting layout of HT leads in the distributor. If you are a stickler for originality, you'll want to preserve such features after a rebuild, so don't lose anything, or lose a record of what fits where

way they say the numbers. They will call 14/0.30 fourteen-thirty, and 14/012 fourteen-oh-one-two. I will deal with the various sizes of cable you need for different circuits, and the colour codings, in the chapter on rewiring.

All cables should be finished with a proper terminal. Twisting the wires into a loop is the hallmark of a bodger, and only ensures future trouble. You'll be offered two sorts of terminals, crimp-on and solder types. The crimp-on sort are usually offered in various sizes in a box complete with an attractive looking multi-purpose tool which claims to be a crimper, insulation stripper, wire cutter and 'bolt cropper' all in one. The terminals are often fitted with hard plastic sleeves. Some people like them, but I don't. The squashed-out sleeve doesn't make a very attractive-looking job, and though crimping is a perfectly good method of attaching terminals to cables when it's done on a production machine, I've yet to find a hand crimper that guarantees a first-class attachment every time. Indeed, I've known quite a few home restorers have electrical troubles which were traced, eventually, to a bad connection inside a crimped-on terminal which looked fine—until you pulled hard.

Even though some cars had special plinths, many electrical items were standardised designs, and found their way into many different cars in the 1950s and 1960s. These are Lucas stop/tail, and indicator lamps, but AC Delco, and the other European concerns, all took this business to a fine art. Restoration, therefore, becomes easier, if you scout around for parts from other cars

My advice is to go for the soldered type of terminal and separate sleeves. It takes longer but it's certain. Always use a non-corroding resin-cored solder, the sort made for radio and similar electronic work, and do not use liquid fluxes for electrical work. They are fine for general soldering where you can scrub down the job afterwards with hot water and soda, but most of them are 'killed spirits'—hydrochloric acid with zinc dissolved in it— and the slightest trace left behind will turn the work green and horrible in a very short time.

Soldering is such a simple job when it's done the right way, but so many people make heavy going of it. There are two golden rules for success. The first is that the parts to be joined together must be absolutely clean, and the second is to tin the two components with solder and *then* sweat them together. Take soldering a terminal as an example. Tin the bared wire by holding the soldering iron against it and touching the strands—not the iron—with the solder till it flows, and hold the iron there for a moment or two to make sure the solder flows properly. If you hold the solder against the iron it will melt more quickly, and appear to flow on to the wire, but the wire will not be hot enough for it to bond properly and you will get a high-resistance joint, usually known as a 'dry' joint. Go through the same procedure with the terminal, having first cleaned the wire trough with a folded slip of emery paper. Then put the wire in the terminal, fold over the tags with a pair of pliers, and hold the iron against it till the solder inside the tags melts and flows. That way you get a perfect joint with a low resistance, approaching zero.

If you need to join two lengths of cable, as for instance if you are partly rewiring back into a loom, either solder the two cables together and use a sleeve, or use the small fold-over type of plastic jointing box made by 3M and Lucas. This has a notched steel plate which bites through the insulation so you don't have to strip the end of the cable. These joining boxes are also very useful for taking a branch feed off the middle of another cable run.

If you join two cables by soldering, you will have to cover the join somehow, to avoid electrical shorting. Plastic insulation tape is one way, but it doesn't look very neat, nor very professional. It is better to use a sleeve, but here you have the problem of keeping the sleeve in place. If it is large enough to slide on, it will slide off again. A neat solution is to use old-fashioned rubber valve tubing from a cycle shop. You might have to search around for it, but it *is* still made. Cut a length, thread a piece of stiff wire through it and roll the tubing down till it looks like a small doughnut. Roll this on the end of the cable and, when the join is soldered, unroll it over the join.

Often you will want to thread several lengths of cable through a piece of pvc plastic sleeving to make things neater or to protect the cables under the wing of the car. Thread them through before you solder the terminals on. The first few go through all right, but they soon get more and more awkward till one sticks halfway. To overcome this you can use an aerosol spray of silicone lubricant. I haven't seen it in many auto accessory shops, but if you have difficulty try one of the shops that cater for professional wiring contractors. As well as lubricating, it helps to keep water out. If you can't get it, use one of the all-purpose lubricants-cum-water-dispersants such as WD-40. Never pass cables, sleeved or unsleeved, through

Do not despair if your car lacks some electrical items. Careful searching at autojumbles or swop meets often helps you stock up again

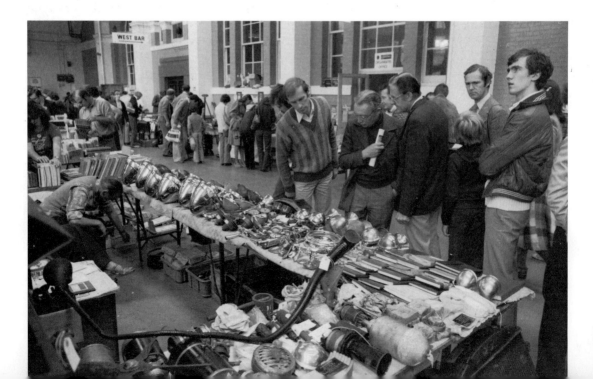

holes in metal panels without using a grommet, and remember to thread the grommet over the end of the sleeve after the cables are in but before you solder on the terminals, otherwise you might not be able to fit it on.

I've left until last the most useful and essential piece of equipment in your electrical toolbox: the meter. There are some very cheap and cheerful moving-iron meters about, with colourful descriptions on the box that lead you to believe they will do anything in the way of diagnosing faults, short of putting them right. Don't believe it. This type of cheap meter, usually originating in the Far East, may be all right for checking torch batteries, but as a meter for setting up a voltage control unit it is quite useless.

Not all meters from the Far East are rubbish, but make sure you get a good quality moving coil model or an accurate digital read-out model, and make sure it covers all the ranges you are likely to want. Some meters are restricted in their ranges, and are intended for specific rather than general use. Look after your meter and it will serve you well for years.

Remember to 'tin' the wire and the connector before finally soldering up a connection, and this will help you not to burn the insulation as well

If you have, or are thinking of getting, an engine diagnostic instrument, it will probably have the low and high ranges of volts, ohms and amps that you need. If not, try a shop that caters for radio builders and enthusiasts. You won't need to buy the most expensive meter they can offer because you are not dealing in fractions of a milliamp like the electronic specialists. You need a robust one with a reasonable internal resistance, say 30,000 ohms/volt DC, and which will read from zero to 20 volts, zero to 50 amps and zero to 1 kilo-ohm, with switching to high and low ranges, so that you can read accurately to at least a quarter-volt, quarter-ohm and quarter-amp right across the range. Make sure it is the sort which gives a full-scale deflection on the ohms scale, in other words there is zero resistance, when you put the two probes together. You will be using this setting often to check for continuity and perfect joints.

As well as the tools I've mentioned you will find uses for small instrument screwdrivers, a hydrometer, a battery charger and a few 'special tools' you can make yourself, but I will deal with these as we come to them.

Chapter 2 | Looking after your battery

The battery is the heart of the car's electrical system, and it is quite an expensive item, so it pays, literally, to look after it, as well as lessening the chance of being let down on a cold, wet morning.

It doesn't ask much, only that it be kept clean, kept topped up (unless it is one of the later maintenance-free types), and used regularly. This last requirement is often overlooked by people taking on the complete rebuild of a car. They stand a perfectly good battery to one side, forget about it for a year or more and then wonder why it lets them down. If you are laying up the car for anything longer than two or three months, either ask a friend if he will use your battery on his car, alternating, say, every fortnight with his own, or give it a regular discharge and slow recharge. The easiest way to discharge it is to connect a headlamp bulb across it, using a pair of leads and crocodile clips (you can even use it as a portable lead light). The recharge should be on the lowest setting of your charger.

The electrolyte inside your battery is dilute sulphuric acid, and the level drops because of evaporation. Only the water content of the electrolyte evaporates, so despite the bottles of 'topping-up liquid' offered in some accessory shops, all you need to add, provided you haven't spilled any of the electolyte, is distilled or de-ionised water. If you have spilt some, seek the advice of a battery specialist for the strength of new electrolyte you need. Some people will tell you that if you live in a soft water area you can safely top up with tap water, but I would not advise it. Tap water is 'pure' to drink, but it may contain chlorine and possibly fluoride compounds, neither of which does the battery any good. Melted frost from a refrigerator or freezer is better, but distilled water in bulk is so cheap, especially when compared to the price of a new battery, that it is not worth bothering with alternatives. If you have the type of battery where you can see inside the cells, the electrolyte should be seen to reach between an eighth and a quarter of an inch above the top of the plates.

Keep the top of the battery dry, and the terminals clean. If the battery has been neglected and started to grow green or white sulphate crystals, clean these off with hot water, and wire brush the terminals and posts clean. Sometimes you will find a hard grey deposit on the terminal posts which is hard to shift with a wire brush but which comes off readily enough with fine emery cloth. The trouble is that after several cleanings in this way, the taper on the post becomes smaller and the normal hooded type of lead terminal refuses to tighten down.

In the hints and tips columns of some magazines I have seen it advised that you should cut a slice off the bottom of the terminal so that it doesn't hit the battery. At best, this is a temporary cure. Before long the post bottoms on the inside of the terminal and appears tight, even though it is not making good contact. Filing the top of the battery post is even worse. The proper answer is to change the terminals for the older, clamp-on type. There is no need to solder them on to the cables, for the two holding screws on the shank of the terminal are quite adequate. To prevent

The only proper way to test the state of charge of a battery is to use a hydrometer

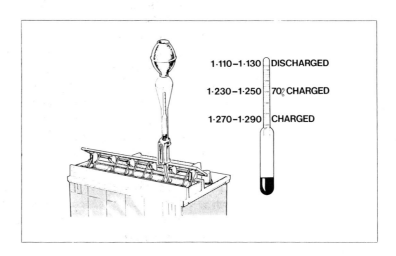

1·110–1·130 DISCHARGED

1·230–1·250 70% CHARGED

1·270–1·290 CHARGED

Below **Looks nasty, doesn't it?
Many batteries get into this state,
and you must get rid of all the
corrosion around the terminals,
repair all damaged cell plugs,
and get rid of all condensation.
Leave that '+' sign on the casing,
to remind you of the system's
polarity**

Right **Old-fashioned battery
terminal clamps like these are to
be preferred to the dome types,
which may not seat properly, so if
you are not too intent on
originality, I recommend that
you acquire some. Always keep
them clamped up tight, and keep
them clean and dry**

sulphate forming again, you can buy special impregnated washers to fit over the terminal posts, but a method just as effective and certainly well proven, is to coat the post and terminal with petroleum jelly (Vaseline). Do not use ordinary grease as this can form a resistance.

The only really accurate way to check the state of charge of a battery is to measure the specific gravity of the electrolyte with a hydrometer. In some accessory shops you may find testers like a small syringe which have floating balls of different colours to indicate 'good', 'indifferent' and 'low'. They are better than nothing, but a proper hydrometer with a calibrated scale is better still. The specific gravity of the electrolyte in a fully charged cell will be 1.270 to 1.290. A reading between 1.230 and 1.250 means it is about three quarters charged, and ought to be able to start the car. Between 1.110 and 1.130 means it is flat.

Strictly speaking the readings ought to be corrected for

temperature, but for practical purposes these figures will give you a good idea of the battery's state of health. A more important factor than the fine accuracy of the reading is that it should be almost the same for all the cells in the battery. If one cell gives a consistently lower reading than all the others, it is a pretty safe bet that this particular cell is nearing the end of its life, the most common cause of a battery failing to hold its charge.

A survey carried out by Lucas showed that in Britain, in winter, because of cold starts and earlier lighting-up times, plus the extra load of heaters, demisters and so on, most batteries in cars spend the winter only 70 per cent charged at best. Most car manufacturers choose a size of battery for the car that will give a good starter cranking speed at about 7 degrees below freezing, when it is only 70 per cent charged. The capacities of batteries are quoted in ampere-hours, usually at a 10 hour rate or a 20 hour rate. The slower the rate of discharge the greater the capacity. To compare the two ratings, multiply the 10 hour rate by 8/7 to get the 20 hour rate, or conversely multiply the 20 hour rate by 7/8 to get the 10 hour rate.

If you are buying a new battery it is important to get one of at least the same capacity as the one originally specified. You can keep your battery fully charged in winter with an inexpensive home charger, but remember to loosen the cell filler caps before switching on. When a battery is being charged it gives off hydrogen gas which is easily ignited (remember the airship *Hindenburg*?) so always switch off at the mains before connecting or disconnecting the clips from the battery posts, keep the battery away from naked flames, including easily forgotten heaters, and don't smoke over it. If you ignite the hydrogen the battery could, quite literally, explode. I've seen the results, and they are not pleasant. The latest maintenance-free batteries never need topping up. They are completely sealed. The plates contain less antimony than ordinary batteries, and give off far less hydrogen. They are quite safe to charge at home, despite what you might have read, provided you follow the manufacturer's instructions and are careful not to exceed the stated maximum charging current, so get a charger with an ammeter built in.

Chapter 3 | Dynamos

Your car will be fitted either with a dynamo or alternator, an alternator being found on more modern examples. The dynamo is sometimes called the generator, but in this book I shall stick to the word dynamo.

Older dynamos, mostly of prewar vintage, had three carbon brushes, the third brush being moveable to control the output. It was, at best, a rather crude form of control, and though it persisted for a short time after the war, it soon gave way to the system I shall describe here, the shunt-wound type of dynamo with an automatic control box. I shall also deal mainly with Lucas equipment, because it is very typical of the type, but if you have a dynamo of other make, stay with me because the principles of checking and overhaul will be much the same.

Before you start stripping the dynamo to cure a low or non-existent electrical charge, it is as well to check the belt drive. Many cases of faulty dynamos and alternators turn out to be due to a loose or slipping drive belt.

If tightening the belt doesn't cure the trouble, there is a simple spot check you can make on a dynamo. Remove the two cables from the terminals F and D on the dynamo and mark them so that they can be put back in their correct places. Often they are of different sizes, but if you make a mistake and connect them the wrong way round you will burn out the points in the control box and possibly the dynamo field coils as well. It is sound practice to mark all cables to avoid any chance of confusion.

With the cables disconnected and held well out of the way, bridge the two terminals on the dynamo with a bare piece of wire, and connect the voltmeter between this bridge and a chassis earth. Start the engine and rev it very

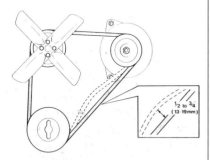

Many apparent charging problems can be traced to a worn or slack fanbelt. Always check for this, but do not strain it up tight or you will overload the dynamo bearing. There should be about half to three quarters of an inch movement on the longest run of the belt

Left **It helps to hold the pulley still while you undo the nut, by gripping it in an old fanbelt held in the vice**

Below left **Despite its looks, the windings on this dynamo armature checked out perfectly, but the commutator needed cleaning and undercutting where the slots were filled with dust from the brushes**

Below **The end plate of a two-brush dynamo. The brushes and springs are simple to replace**

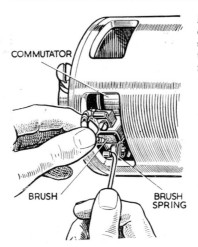

Make a small hook from a piece of wire to hold the dynamo brush springs back; it makes lifting out the brushes for inspection very much easier

COMMUTATOR

BRUSH

BRUSH SPRING

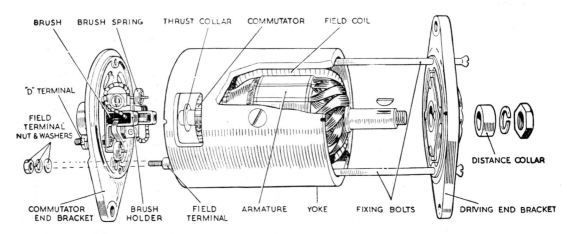

BRUSH   BRUSH SPRING   THRUST COLLAR   COMMUTATOR   FIELD COIL

"D" TERMINAL

FIELD TERMINAL NUT & WASHERS

DISTANCE COLLAR

COMMUTATOR END BRACKET   BRUSH HOLDER   FIELD TERMINAL   ARMATURE   YOKE   FIXING BOLTS   DRIVING END BRACKET

The components of a dynamo. The bearing at the commutator end is usually a plain bronze bush, but at the drive end where it has to take the pull of the fanbelt, a ballrace is fitted and is usually held by a riveted plate. This must be replaced with steel, not aluminium rivets or it will come loose in service and give endless trouble

gently. Do not run the engine fast because the dynamo is running almost entirely without load, and too high a speed can damage it electrically. Keep the voltage below 20 volts on a 12 volt system, or 10 volts on a 6 volt system. The needle of the voltmeter should remain steady. If it flickers badly, or you get a very low reading, the dynamo needs attention.

Most dynamos come apart quite easily, the awkward part usually being to hold the pulley while you undo its nut. The easy way is to run an old fan belt round it and clamp the belt in a vice. With the nut loose, the pulley can then be taken off with a puller. The pulley is usually located by a half-moon Woodruff key, which has to come out

TESTING THE ARMATURE CIRCUIT

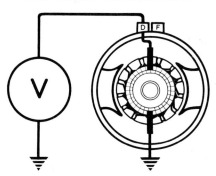

SPEED _____ 1200-1500 R.P.M.
READING _____ 1·5 - 2·0 V

TESTING THE FIELD CIRCUIT

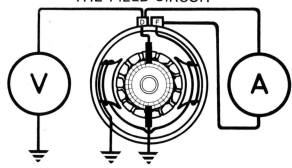

VOLTMETER READING NOMINAL BATTERY VOLTAGE
AMMETER READING _____ FIELD CURRENT 2A.

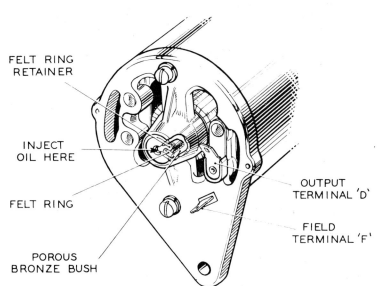

FELT RING RETAINER

INJECT OIL HERE

FELT RING

POROUS BRONZE BUSH

OUTPUT TERMINAL 'D'

FIELD TERMINAL 'F'

Above **To check the armature circuit connect a volt meter between terminal D, the output terminal on the dynamo, and a chassis earth. Rev the engine to charging speed, when you should see a reading between 1.5 and 2 volts. If there is no reading, or if the reading increases as the revs rise, the dynamo needs taking apart for examination. You can use a headlamp bulb instead of a volt meter. It will glow dimly if all is well but either fail to light, or shine brightly, if the dynamo needs overhaul.**
To check the field circuit without taking the dynamo off the car, you need a separate volt meter and ammeter. With engine running and the voltmeter reading battery voltage, the ammeter should read about 2 amps. A higher or lower reading indicates trouble in the dynamo

Left **Pre-war Lucas dynamos had a grease nipple on the end bearing but soon after the war this was replaced by a felt pad to hold oil. A common cause of wear is failure to lubricate the pad. It should be given a squirt of engine oil about every 6000 miles or so**

A problem on many cars is that the dynamo has to live close to hot engine parts. How many Jaguar XK120s suffered dynamo failure because they were close to the cast exhaust manifolds in a hot engine bay?

before the shaft will go through the bearing. Many people make a tremendous meal of taking out this key, with pliers and grips. The simple way is to put a blunt screwdriver under one end and give it a sharp tap.

The rest of the dynamo comes apart after you take the nuts and washers off the field terminal, usually the smaller one of the two that are present, and undo the two long through-bolts that hold the end plates together. Some makes of dynamo have a ball bearing at the drive end and a bronze bush at the commutator end, others have a ball bearing at each end, the one at the commutator end is often held in place by a thrust screw. Whichever type you have, take care not to lose any small springs, washers or distance pieces when you pull the plates apart. and if any small pieces are loose, make a note of where they fit.

If the ball bearings are in good condition there is no need to disturb them, but if they feel sloppy or gritty they need to be renewed. On some makes these push straight out of

Riley didn't build in much space around their 2.4-litre 'Big Four' engine, and the engine bay of the Healey Silverstone, which used the engine at the end of the 1940s, was restricted as well. The distributor was close to the dynamo, and both were close to the front SU carburettor. Dynamo adjustment, however, should be straightforward enough, *if* you can reach the lower fixing bolts!

their housing, but on others they are held by a cover plate and rivets. Under the cover plate there will probably be a corrugated washer, a flat washer and an oil retaining washer. Once again, make a note of the order in which they fit. Pack the new bearing with high melting point grease before you press it in, and use new rivets—steel not aluminium—to replace the cover plate.

If there is a bronze bush in the commutator end bracket, try the fit of the armature. If it wobbles, the bush needs renewing. If the armature bearing surface is damaged, though this is less usual, the armature is useless, and *should be changed*. Sometimes you can get new armatures from an agent, and I have even seen them on autojumble stalls, but always take the old one along to check that the new one is *exactly* the same. If a new armature is unobtainable, the best thing is to button everything up again and exchange the dynamo for a reconditioned unit. If it really is a rare model, and an exchange one cannot be found, the

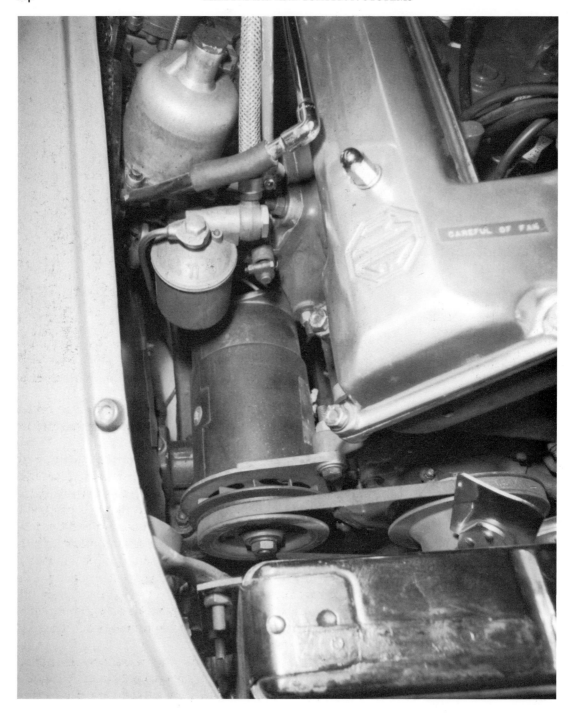

Right I removed the HT lead from No. 1 plug, in this shot, to demonstrate the fixing of the Lucas dynamo to the cylinder block. If you are sure such fittings were original, preserve them after the rebuild

Opposite This is the engine bay of an MGA Twin Cam. Getting at the dynamo isn't going to be easy at the best of times, but when the engine is hot...

only answer is to get someone with a lathe to turn down the bearing surface and make you a new, undersize bronze bush, but this really is a last resort.

The bronze bush may have a blind cover over it, and though there are special maker's tools to extract it, you can pull it out quite easily if you find a tap to screw in—$\frac{5}{8}$ in. (15 mm) on most Lucas dynamos—so that you can get a pull at it. The new bush should be soaked in light engine oil for 24 hours, but if you are in a hurry, stand it in a tin of oil in a bath of boiling water for a couple of hours. If you push it into place when dry it will probably fail within six months. Under the bush will be a washer, or washers, and a felt lubricating pad. Put enough oil on the new pad to make it wet, but not so much that it runs out all over the armature.

The armature will probably be blackened, or at least badly discoloured. It can be cleaned with a petrol-moistened rag or a strip of fine glass paper. Use glass paper rather than emery or wet and dry rubbing paper, because the carborundum particles on these are conductors and they can bed into the separators between the armature segments, and short things out. If the commutator is pitted or burnt, or if the old brushes have worn grooves into it, a light skim on a lathe will restore it, but take care not to reduce the diameter below the minimum specified by the maker. If you do, there is a danger that as the brushes wear they will drop out of their holders, and jam. The insulating separators between the segments of the commutator should be undercut to about $\frac{3}{32}$ in. (0.8 mm) deep, with a hacksaw blade ground down to the insulator thickness. Try to cut them square and not vee-shaped, and take-off the burrs the undercutting will raise with fine sandpaper.

Fitting new brushes to a dynamo is usually quite straightforward

Short circuits on the turns of the armature that are not obvious cannot be checked adequately without using an instrument known as a growler, which is seldom found outside dynamo repair workshops, but this fault is comparatively rare and need only be suspected if the armature windings look black and burnt. If two adjacent segments on the commutator are burnt, often with a flattened look, this is a sign of an open circuit somewhere in the windings. In either case you need a new armature, or a replacement (exchange) dynamo.

The inside of the yoke, the main body of the dynamo, will no doubt be full of black dust from worn brushes. Since this is a good conductor, clean it out with a stiff bristle brush. To test the field coils, the large insulated windings inside the yoke, connect an ohm meter between the field terminal and a clean part of the yoke. You should get a reading of 6 to 6.2 ohms. If the meter reads infinity (which means there is no electrical contact at all between the field and the yoke), there is a break somewhere in the field windings. If it reads considerably lower than 6 ohms the insulation is breaking down. Before you discard a yoke for this reason, check the insulating plate that prevents the junction of the field coils from touching the inside of the yoke. Sometimes dust from worn brushes collects behind this and shorts across.

Above **Undercutting the insulation between segments of the dynamo's commutator. This should not be done, however, for starter motors**

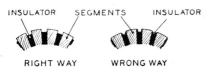

Above **Right and wrong ways to undercut the dynamo armature. Always try to cut square grooves, rather than vee-shapes**

Right **Checking the battery terminal voltage under load conditions—a typical petrol engine figure should be 10 volts**

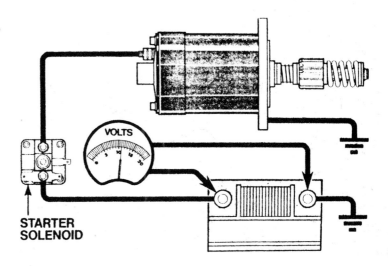

STARTER SOLENOID

Replacing field coils is definitely a job for the maker's service agent or auto-electrician of some clout, whatever you might have read elsewhere. The screws which hold the pole pieces are put in with a large power driver to a torque figure you will never achieve by hand, and you need a special expander to hold the pole pieces while you replace the screws and tighten them, once again to a very high torque.

Worn carbon brushes should be replaced, and the new brushes checked for freedom in their holders. If necessary, ease them with a fine file. If the brush springs feel weak, they too should be replaced. You can obtain most dynamo parts from the maker's agents. They will probably suggest you buy a new or reconditioned unit, but so far as I can find out, parts are listed and priced for most makes, so provided they are in stock you ought to be able to get them.

When you put the dynamo together it will help if you lift the brushes in their holders, and wedge them with the side of the spring so that they stay clear of the armature. If there are inspection windows in the yoke you can unhook the springs with a piece of wire after the armature is home, but if there are no windows you will have to reach in with your wire hook and lift the springs into position as soon as the brushes are over the armature.

A rebuilt dynamo, either an exchange unit or one you have rebuilt yourself, has to be polarized to match the system of the car (negative or positive earth) to which it is fitted. New and exchange dynamos are suitable for either polarity and should be polarized after you have taken delivery.

Polarizing a dynamo is very simple. All you have to do is mount it on the engine so that the yoke is earthed, and take a cable from the live (non-earthed) terminal of the battery. Hold this cable against the dynamo field terminal for a few seconds. When you take it off there will be a fuzzy blue flash, and the dynamo will be polarized to suit the car. It can be done beforehand with a battery and two leads, but if you wait until it is fitted you are certain of getting it polarized the right way round. *Never* attempt to polarize an alternator. You will surely ruin it.

Chapter 4 | **Alternators**

Alternators took over from dynamos in the 1960s and 1970s as a more efficient way of providing charging current, particularly at low engine revs. Many people who will tackle a dynamo rebuild fight shy of stripping an alternator because it contains electronic parts—transistors and diodes—and you need a soldering iron to change the diode pack. But there is no need to approach an alternator with trepidation. Provided you go about things in an orderly way it is, if anything, easier than a dynamo to overhaul.

With an alternator there are a few things you must never do. *Never* disconnect the battery while the engine is running, and never run the engine with the alternator leads disconnected. And, if you do any electric welding or brazing on the car, disconnect both the battery and the alternator before you start.

Electrically, the main difference between a dynamo and an alternator is the method of changing the alternating current (AC) each produces to the direct current (DC) needed to charge the battery. With a dynamo this is done by the segments of the commutator, but an alternator has a plain slip ring to pick up the current so diodes—electrical one-way valves—are also needed to change the AC to DC. Early alternators had an external control box, a field isolating relay and a warning light control. On later alternators these are all grouped together inside the unit, so there are no external bits and pieces to worry about.

Typical of the two types are the Lucas AC series, such as the AC 10 and AC 11, which need external components, and the ACR models where they are built in. If you have trouble with one of the earlier AC models it is worthwhile changing over to the later ACR, unless you are a stickler for originality. You may be able to exchange an AC for an ACR, but not many agents are keen to do this, so you may have to get a secondhand one, and overhaul it. You can work out the changes in wiring from any wiring diagram using an ACR.

There are a number of checks you can make on an ACR alternator before you take it off the car. Indeed, without a test bench you cannot check it properly once it is removed. Take the plastic end cover off and reconnect the cables. If the warning light on the dash stays on when the engine is running, the chances are that the surge protection diode has failed. This is separate from the main rectifier diode pack and can be renewed by itself. Disconnect it and take it out—only one small bolt must be removed—and try again. If the warning light now goes out, the surge pro-

Early Lucas alternators were of the AC type which had to be used with a relay. The wiring varied, depending on whether the car had a negative or positive earth system, so check the circuit diagram in the handbook

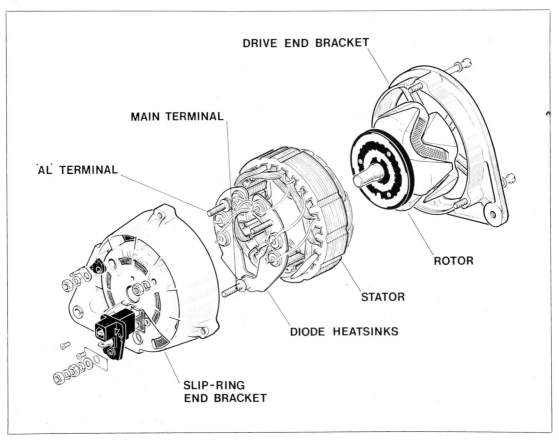

DRIVE END BRACKET

MAIN TERMINAL

'AL' TERMINAL

ROTOR

STATOR

DIODE HEATSINKS

SLIP-RING
END BRACKET

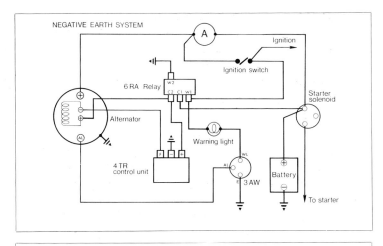

The basic wiring circuit for a Lucas AC alternator on a negative earth system

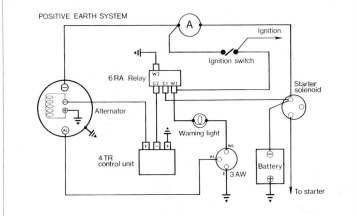

The theoretical circuit for a Lucas AC alternator with positive earth system

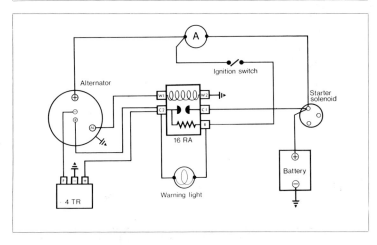

Towards the end of their run, Lucas AC alternators used a different type of relay, the 15RA which simplified the wiring because there was no need for a separate warning light control—a component which often gave trouble

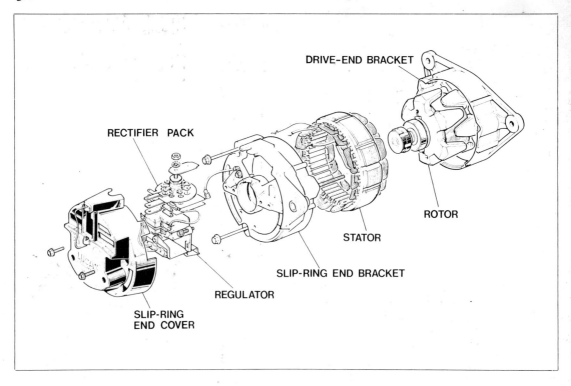

DRIVE-END BRACKET

RECTIFIER PACK

ROTOR

STATOR

SLIP-RING END BRACKET

REGULATOR

**SLIP-RING
END COVER**

**The Lucas ACR alternator did
not need external control
components, and was more
reliable than the AC models**

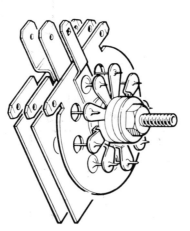

**The rectifier pack has to be
replaced as a unit if any of the 9
diodes fail. It is unwise to try to
replace individual diodes as you
could so easily damage the others**

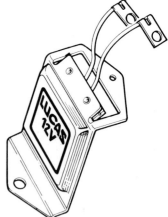

**The internal voltage regulator on
an ACR alternator is a simple
sealed unit**

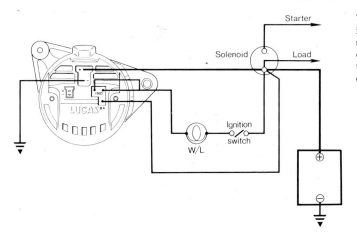

When the ACR was first introduced it used a battery sensing system. This can be checked by looking at the terminals because there are five connections

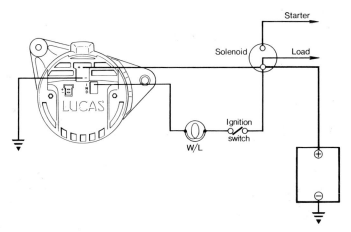

On the later machine sensing systems there were only three terminals, though the alternator still had two connecting blocks

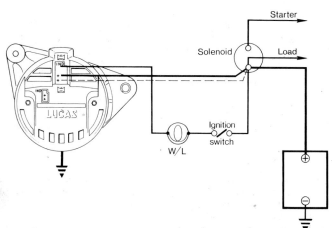

The latest ACR alternators have only one connecting block

Just occasionally, there is room to work on electrical components of complex cars. On this Ferrari 365GTB/4 Daytona, the alternator is easy to see, and adjust—and it ought to keep cool as well

tection diode was faulty. Some alternators have a built-in radio suppressor. If this has failed, the wire that connects it to the brush housing will probably be burnt. Once again, replacement is easy. If the warning light flickers or comes on intermittently, it means the brushes are worn or the slip ring has glazed. These can usually be renewed without taking the alternator off the car, and it pays to do this as soon as you notice the fault. Worn brushes can damage the main rectifier pack, which is much more expensive than a set of brushes.

The last check with the alternator still in place is to the regulator. Once again the symptom is irregular operation of the warning light. To check the regulator, first disconnect the surge protection diode, then earth the body of the regulator to the alternator housing. The warning light

Vee-8 engines might be bulky, but sometimes the hang-on components are well placed. It would be a pleasure to work on this alternator, mounted high up on the Chevrolet's vee-8 unit

should not come on at all. If it does, renew the regulator as a unit. Check also for continuity and good connections of all the cables leading to the alternator, and that the body of the alternator is properly earthed through the mounting bracket.

Different alternators take apart in different ways, but this is usually apparent when you look at them. On most components there is a plastic cover over the slip ring end, and you may need a small socket screwdriver to take this off. The two end brackets, at the slip ring end and the drive end, are held together by long bolts which may fit from the slip ring end *or* the drive end. Sometimes there are lock nuts, sometimes not.

On the type with a large plastic end cover, most of the parts which are likely to give trouble can be reached without dismantling the alternator any further. The carbon brushes are carried in a nylon housing, and although you can change the brushes just by undoing the small screws at the top, it is better to take the housing right off so that you can check the condition of the slip ring. Before you can take the housing off you have to undo the lead to the surge protection diode, the small unit which generally sits beside the rectifier pack. Taking out the rectifier pack involves unsoldering three wires. These rectifier packs are the most expensive parts of an alternator, so take care not to damage one when you take it out, just in case it doesn't have to be renewed.

The most likely way to damage the rectifier pack is to get the wires too hot while unsoldering it. To avoid such damage use a pair of pointed-nosed pliers to hold the wire between the pack and the connection while you solder or unsolder it. The pliers act as a heat sink to draw the heat away from the diodes. With the leads unsoldered (make a note of where each one fitted) the rectifier pack can be taken out after undoing its holding screw.

The slip ring will probably be discoloured, but will clean up with the aid of a petrol-moistened rag. If it is glazed, use fine sandpaper as for the commutator of a dynamo. After cleaning, check it for continuity and insulation. To check for continuity set your meter to 'ohms' and test across from the centre spindle to the track where the car-

Exploded view of the construction of any early type of Lucas 11AC alternator, for which the rectifier pack was separately mounted, and is not shown here

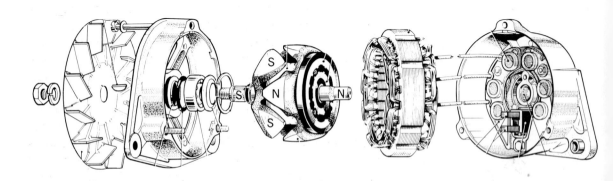

bon brushes run. You should get a perfect connection, no resistance at all. The check for insulation is to connect your meter between the centre spindle and the casing of the alternator. Here you should get an infinity reading, which means no electrical connection at all.

If you find the slip ring badly worn or if either of the two tests shows it is faulty, you can renew it quite easily. Mark across the two end caps and the centre pack of laminations, as a guide to putting them together again in the same relative position, undo the main body bolts and lift off the slip ring cover. On most alternators the slip ring can be prised off the rotor shaft after unsoldering the two connections. The new (replacement) ring may include a leaf spring, which was not fitted to many early models.

Check the diodes in the rectifier pack either with your ohm meter or with a lamp and battery. As these are electrical one-way valves they should pass current one way, but show high resistance in the other direction. You will not get a perfect connection one way because the resistance of a diode varies according to the voltage across it, and there is only a small battery in your ohm meter. *Never* use the type of ohm meter with a hand-cranked generator to test diodes. You will blow them. If you use a lamp and battery, keep the wattage of the bulb down to 1.5—a small dash panel warning light is perfect. You will have great difficulty in buying diodes separately, so if one is faulty you will have to renew the whole pack.

The last electrical check is for continuity of the stator windings. With the ohm meter you should get continuity through any of the wires, taken in any combination.

The bearings of most alternators are easier to replace than those of most dynamos. The drive end bearing is invariably a ball race, and though on some earlier models it may be held by a riveted plate, on most later models there is only a plate and circlip. As a rule there are no ears on the circlip, so lever it out with a small screwdriver in the depression in the side of the housing. The rear bearing is probably a needle roller, much easier to replace than a bronze bush, but it seldom gives trouble because it is so lightly loaded. Usually all that is needed is to clean and repack it with high melting point grease.

Chapter 5 | **Starter motors**

Overhauling a starter motor is much the same task as overhauling a dynamo except that there are more brushes and a drive mechanism to cope with. The starter will be one of two types, inertia drive (where the first spin of the motor sends the pinion into engagement with the flywheel) and pre-engaged (where the pinion is taken into engagement with the flywheel before the main starting torque comes in).

I will deal with inertia drives first. These will be one of two types. Either there will be a castellated nut and split pin holding the drive pinion to the end of the shaft or there will be a circlip. The split-pinned type presents no problem—other than remembering that the nut is usually left-hand-thread—but with the circlip type you will need a compressor to take the tension off the circlip before you remove it. These compressors are quite cheap, and it is not worth the trouble of trying to make do with makeshift clamps or grips.

Make a careful note of the order in which all the pieces of the drive lift off the shaft so you can put them back in the right order and the right way round. Wash them in paraffin and inspect them for burrs. If you find any, smooth them off with a fine file. Most people will say that you should reassemble the drive components dry, and certainly any old sticky oil will stop them from working properly. Lucas, however, recommend that the helix should be lubricated with Molykiron SAE 5 oil, and the straight splines with Shell SB 2628 grease, or their equivalents. Do not overdo either. On some inertia drive motors there is a small antirattle spring which is quite weak but which, if it gets bent, can jam in the helix and stop it working

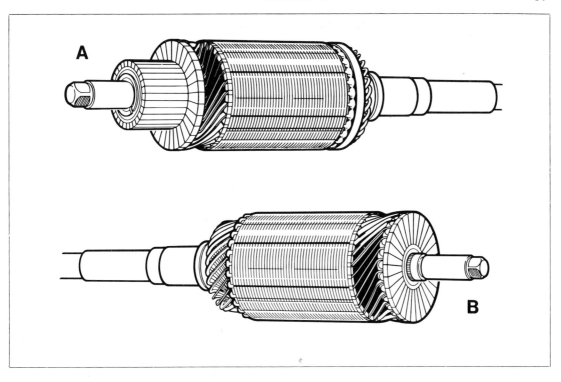

Above **Most dynamos will have the barrel type commutator (A) but some exchange units may have a face type (B)**

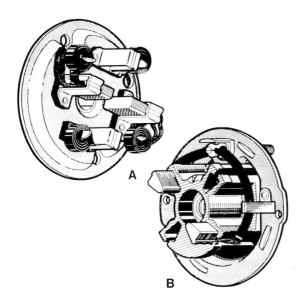

Left **The two types of end plate to match the two types of commutator**

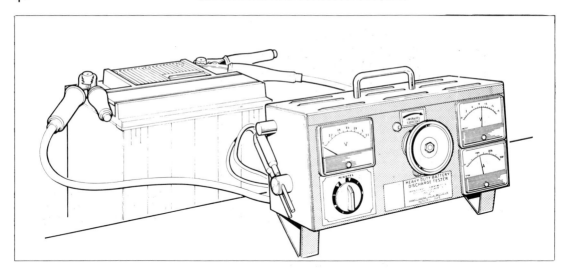

Checking the battery voltage on load. It should not drop below 10 volts

or, worse, hold it jammed into engagement with the fly-wheel. Should this happen, and if the engine starts, switch off as quickly as possible or the starter will burn out. Some garages will tell you that these small springs are unobtainable by themselves, but if you find a friendly agent he will most likely have a selection from which you can choose one to suit the drive.

The bearings, commutator and brushes are dealt with in much the same way as those in a dynamo except that the commutator must *not* be undercut on a starter motor, and there are usually two bronze bushes for the armature instead of one bronze and one ball bearing. Two of the starter's brushes are fixed to the commutator end plate, and two go to the field coils. These last two have the ends of their leads spot welded in place. They are welded to a common junction on a series-wound motor, and to the ends of the field coils on a series-parallel motor. Apart from this difference you need not worry whether the motor is series or series-parallel. You will never undo the spot welds satisfactorily, but the easy way out when you are renewing brushes is to cut the leads of the old brushes about half an inch to an inch from the spot welded join and then solder the leads of the new brushes to the old leads.

Checking the field coil continuity and insulation is a different procedure on a starter, compared with a dynamo,

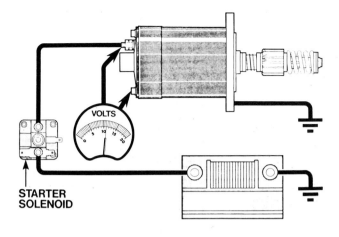

STARTER SOLENOID

The voltage at the starter on load should not be more than half a volt below that at the battery

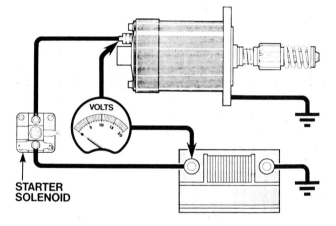

STARTER SOLENOID

With the voltmeter connected as shown, it should register battery voltage before the switch is pressed. When the starter switch is closed the reading should drop to zero. If not, check all the connections

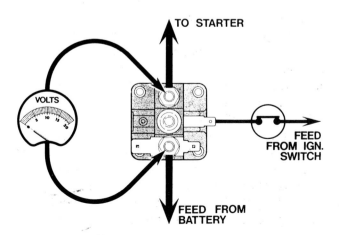

TO STARTER

FEED FROM IGN. SWITCH

FEED FROM BATTERY

You should get similar readings across the solenoid switch as *at the starter switch*—battery voltage with the switch open, zero or near zero with it closed

and depends on the type of winding. If you have the type where the field brushes go to a common junction, test for continuity between the main starter terminal, insulated from the yoke, and the common junction. Test for insulation between the main terminal post and the yoke. If, however, you have the type where the junction for the field

Right **Checking the voltage drop on the earth line. When the solenoid switch is closed the reading should be practically zero**

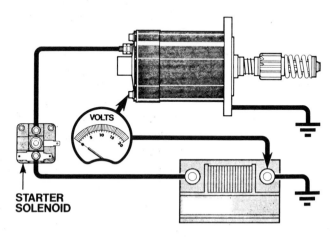

**STARTER
SOLENOID**

Below **With a pre-engaged starter the checks are similar to** *those for an inertia starter* **but remember that with the solenoid on the starter you have to sort out which is the main starter terminal and which are the solenoid terminals**

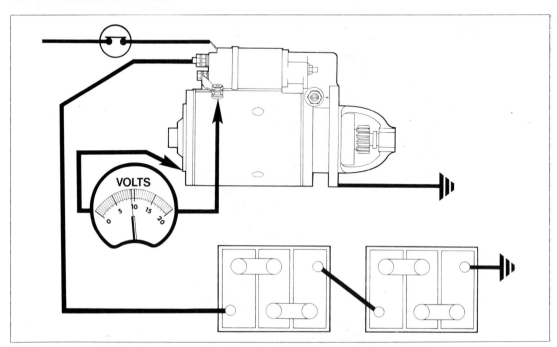

winding is riveted in contact with the yoke, check first for continuity between each brush and a clean part of the yoke. You should get a perfect connection. Then disconnect the riveted connection and check for insulation between each brush and the yoke. If, you get a connection with the rivet disconnected, the windings are shorting to the yoke somewhere along their length and you will never get full power.

When checking for insulation between the field windings and the yoke, a lamp and battery or normal battery driven ohm meter is not sufficient. You should use a mains lamp of 15 watts and at least 100 volts. Please be careful what you are doing. Put the yoke on dry wood or a thick dry rubber mat to insulate it from the bench, and make the connections with crocodile clips before switching on. Prodding about with bare mains leads is a good way of electrocuting yourself. As with a dynamo, special equipment is needed to change the field coils.

When renewing brushes on a starter you must cut the cable and join the new one to it as the cables are spot welded to the field coils

The main cause of this starter not
working was a broken brush
spring on one of the field brushes
(top)

TERMINAL NUTS   THROUGH   COVER   TERMINAL   BEARING
& WASHERS   BOLT   BAND   POST   BUSH

Ⓔ Ⓕ   Ⓓ   Ⓐ   Ⓖ   Ⓡ

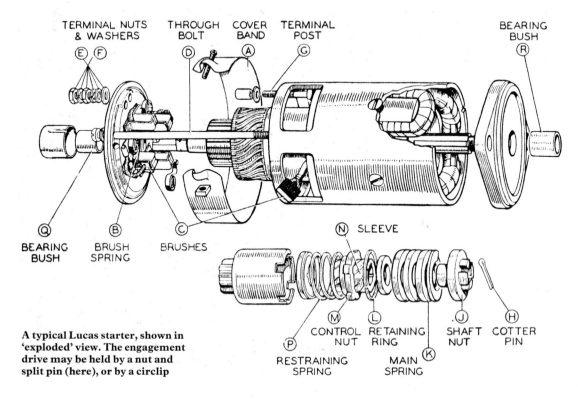

Ⓠ   Ⓑ   Ⓒ   Ⓝ   SLEEVE

BEARING   BRUSH   BRUSHES
BUSH   SPRING

                                    Ⓜ   Ⓛ   Ⓙ   Ⓗ
A typical Lucas starter, shown in   CONTROL   RETAINING   SHAFT   COTTER
'exploded' view. The engagement   Ⓟ   NUT   RING   NUT   PIN
drive may be held by a nut and
split pin (here), or by a circlip   RESTRAINING   MAIN
                                        SPRING   SPRING Ⓚ

The pre-engaged type of starter has a different drive altogether. Engagement of the pinion with the flywheel is by a pivotted lever. The lever may be operated manually via a cable, or electrically via a solenoid. In either case, full current is not supplied to the starter until the drive is firmly in engagement with the flywheel. Pre-engaged starters are usually for heavier duty applications than iner-tia-drive types, and as the pinion does not fly out of engage-ment as soon as the speed of the flywheel is greater than that of the starter drive, there is a clutch on the drive shaft to prevent the flywheel from driving the starter motor.

The task of overhauling the main part of the starter is very similar to overhauling an inertia drive type except that the clutch must be checked. It should engage instantly when turned in one direction, and rotate freely in the other. The term clutch is actually something of a misnomer, as many types are roller-driven freewheels. If washing out with petrol does not cure a sticking or non-engaging

One day you'll need to know that this is a Lucas starter solenoid—and one day you'll hope to find it as accessible as on the Frazer Nash Le Mans Replica!

clutch, the only course is to renew it. Once they are worn they can seldom be repaired satisfactorily.

Usually on pre-engaged starters there is an eccentric pin for the drive operating lever, so that it can be set with its fork end operating smoothly in the collar on the shaft. There is also likely to be a thrust washer on the drive shaft, usually held in place by a circlip. This should be checked for wear and renewed if necessary. All pre-engaged starters with solenoids have to be set up for lost motion between the solenoid and the operating lever, and usually the drive gear has to be set a certain distance from the flywheel when the starter is bolted to the engine. There are so many different types and models it is impossible to detail them here, so you must refer to the car manual or to a service manual published by the starter maker. There is nothing difficult about setting them up, but the methods and figures differ from model to model. Getting the settings correct is important for good starter life and easy action. The solenoid itself can be checked by putting the leads from a battery across it while it is in a vice, but it operates with quite a smack, so make sure it is firmly held.

Looks untidy, doesn't it? But I guess that the starter solenoid was always fixed like this. The extra wiring is because the body shell is in fibreglass, and non-conducting

Chapter 6 | Control boxes

Of all the components on a car with dynamo charging, the control box seems to cause a restorer the most head scratching. It is a prime target for the prod-and-hope merchants, so you may find it well out of adjustment.

There are a number of makes, but only two main types, those with two bobbins for compensated-voltage control and those with three bobbins which are usually current-voltage control. Compensated-voltage control was used before current-voltage control, but just to make things confusing, makers, and more often car manuals, refer to them both as 'CVC' units.

Both types control the output from two or four brush shunt-wound dynamos. The older three brush dynamos merely had a cut-out, but overhauling this is just the same as overhauling the cut-out part of a later control box.

With either type of CVC box, the first thing to do is take it off the bulkhead (firewall) and look at the underside. Inside the base you will find a number of brass or copper connecting straps and some resistors. On some US units by Delco Remy, the resistors may be mounted behind the bobbins. If any of these are burnt, or even blackened, there is not much point in working any further. Such a box has been hopelessly overloaded, or the connections have been made the wrong way round, and it is easier to get another than to try to repair a burnt one.

There are so many detail differences between boxes of different models by the same maker, let alone by different makers, that you will have to refer to a manual for the detail settings. However, they all work on the same principle. The main difference you will come across is in the method of adjustment. On most early US units this is done by bending the bottom tag holding a coil spring running down the back of the bobbin. In most cases you bend the tag down to increase the voltage or current, and up to decrease it. Most later models changed to a screw and an adjuster. As far as I know, all British control boxes have screw adjusters. I shall deal with Lucas units in detail because most of the others follow the same pattern, though the setting figures will be different.

Dealing first with the two-bobbin type of regulator, provided the connecting straps and resistors in the base are all in good condition the next step is to clean and set the points. Start with the points on the voltage regulator, the bobbin with the fewer number of turns. It operates on a very simple principle. A small part of the dynamo's output energises the bobbin so that it becomes an electro-magnet. When the voltage (on a 12 volt system) reaches about 16 volts this magnetism is powerful enough to pull down a rocking arm, generally called the armature. As the armature comes down it opens a pair of contact points, the dynamo stops charging and the magnetism collapses. This allows a spring to pull the armature up again, the points close and the whole cycle is repeated. At normal engine speeds the points open and close far too rapidly to see, but if you rock the armature slowly, with the battery disconnected to be absolutely safe, you can see the action quite clearly.

Voltage regulators on Lucas two-bobbin units will be one of two types. Either the contact points, one of which is adjustable, are at the end of the bobbin facing you when you take the cover off, or they are mounted above the bobbin on top of the frame. On the type which has the contact points at the end of the bobbin, the armature is held by two screws just above the adjustable contact. The voltage regulating screw is on top of the frame just in front of the plastic base.

To get at the points to clean them you can either take the armature out, or you can just take out the adjustable point for refacing on a fine oil stone, and clean the armature point with a strip of emery cloth. After cleaning the points you have to reset the armature. Slacken off the adjustable point, and the voltage regulating screw, and loosen the

The first check on any faulty control box is to look underneath. This box had burnt out because the connection at one end of the large resistor had become unsoldered

armature fixing screws just enough to be able to move the armature. Then put a feeler gauge between the armature and the end of the bobbin. On some Lucas models the feeler should be 0.015 in. (0.38 mm) and on others it may be up to 0.022 in. (0.51 mm), but if you have not got the table of settings use a 0.020 in. feeler (0.050 or 0.051 mm). I have found all the boxes work perfectly well at this setting even though some may not be at their theoretical peak efficiency.

With the feeler in position, hold the armature flat down against it and tighten the fixing screws. Then, with the feeler still in position, screw the adjustable point down until it just meets the armature point. It must meet it fairly and squarely. If it doesn't this means that you have sloped one of the points when you cleaned them. If they meet cleanly, lock the adjustable point and take the feeler away.

On the second type, where the points are mounted above the bobbin, you have to take the armature out to clean them. One of the points is on the armature itself and the

other, the fixed one, is held by two screws to the underside
of the frame. Usually there is a small pack of shims between
the fixed point and the frame to adjust the gap. There is
no need to take the fixed point right out to clean it—you
might drop all the shims. If you slacken the two holding
screws it will swing away from the frame, and you can clean
it with an oilstone.

To reset the armature, put a 0.018 in. (0.46 mm) feeler
between the back of the armature and the regulator frame.
Press the armature back against the feeler and down on
to the bobbin while you tighten the fixing screws.

With the feeler taken out, the gap between the armature
and the top of the bobbin should be between 0.012 in. and
0.020 in. (0.30 to 0.50 mm). If it is outside these limits,
adjust it by adding or removing shims from under the fixed

**A typical Lucas control box with
the voltage regulator on the left
and the cut-out on the right**

point. If you haven't got any spare shims to add, or if there are no shims but just a packing piece, adjust by carefully bending the arm of the fixed point but try to keep the points meeting squarely. *Never* bend the armature to adjust the points gap.

With the gap between the armature and the top of the bobbin within limits, the gap between the points when you push the armature down on to the top of the bobbin should be between 0.006 in. and 0.017 in. (0.15 to 0.40 mm). These are quite generous tolerances, and if you cannot work within them someone has been bending the armature or has taken all the shims out and lost them. In either case look for another unit to cannibalise.

All that remains to be done on the voltage regulator is to adjust the voltage setting screw, but I will deal with this

The only way to adjust the cut-out is by bending the stop-bar above the coil

after discussing the cleaning and adjusting of the cut-out, which is the other bobbin with the greater number of turns of wire.

The cut-out's job is to put the dynamo out of circuit when its output, at low revs, is less than the battery voltage. If this did not happen, the battery would try to motor the dynamo. The cut-out has an electro-magnetic bobbin similar to that on the voltage regulator, and when the dynamo is not charging at a higher voltage than the battery voltage the points of the cut-out are open. When the dynamo builds up its voltage, to about 13 volts on a 12 volt system, the magnet of the cut-out becomes strong enough to pull the armature down and close the points, so putting the dynamo in circuit with the rest of the system.

Clean the cut-out points in position by drawing a strip of emery cloth through them. The points are slightly domed and work with a wiping action which helps to keep them clean. Keep this doming when you clean them, for they should not have flats.

On this control box the voltage regulator points are mounted behind the coil on the frame

On many three-bobbin control boxes, adjustment is by cams. A small tool rather like a drill chuck key is used to operate them

To set the points, first loosen the adjusting screw which is alongside the screw holding the insulated fixed point. Then loosen the armature screws, push the armature squarely in against the end of the bobbin and tighten the screws.

When the armature is pressed against the bobbin the gap between the top face of the armature and the curved stop plate above it should be between 0.025 in, and 0.040 in. (0.65 mm and 1.00 mm). Adjust it by gently bending the arm of the stop plate. When you let the armature go, which means that the points open, the points gap should be set to 0.018 in. (0.45 mm) by bending the arm of the fixed point. When you press the armature against the bobbin after this, the points should close and 'follow through'. That is, the point on the armature should push the fixed point back by anything up to 0.020 in (0.50 mm) after they touch. This gives the wiping action which helps to keep the points clean. It is quite important if the cut-out is to keep its setting for a long period.

With both the voltage regulator and the cut-out cleaned and with their points set, you are now ready to adjust the

A forest of wiring, logically arranged, with a conventional Lucas control box mounted very close to the principal fuses. How often would you find these so ideally placed when the bonnet was raised?

voltage setting. Start by wedging the points of the cut-out closed with a folded strip of paper to put the dynamo in circuit, as you have not yet set the cut-out.

Disconnect the cables from the two terminals marked A and A1 on the regulator box, join them together with a clip and keep them well out of the way where they will not short to earth. Remember whether you have a negative or positive earth system, so that you connect your voltmeter the correct way round, and connect it between terminals D (for dynamo) and E (for Earth). On US regulators these may be labelled G (for generator) and probably GD (for ground). This may vary however, and the equivalents of the D terminal may be labelled A (for armature). To enable you to sort things out whatever the terminals are labelled, disconnect and join together the main feed from the battery or starter solenoid and the cable which feeds from the regulator to the lighting switch. The voltmeter goes between the feed from the dynamo armature and the earth terminal on the regulator. It is as well to check that this terminal is indeed in electrical contact with chassis earth. Sometimes there will be a separate earthing lead from the box, and sometimes it earths through its mounting screws. A bad earth will give you an erratic charging rate and is likely to burn the points.

With the voltmeter connected start the engine and with it running at about half throttle set the voltage adjusting screw to give you a reading of 16 volts on a 12 volt system. This adjustment should be made quite quickly—certainly within half a minute of starting the engine—because with the A and A1 terminals joined together the dynamo is on open circuit and the shunt winding in the control box will soon heat up and give you a false reading. When you stop the engine remember to open the cut-out points again, and reconnect the leads at terminals A and A1.

To adjust the cut-out setting, leave the voltmeter in position, start the engine and screw the cut-out adjusting screw down as the engine is gently revved up from tick-over so that the points click shut when the voltage reaches 13 volts (or 6.5 volts on a 6 volt system). They should open again as the engine dies to tick-over and the voltage drops to between 10 and 8.5 volts (5 to just over 4 volts on a 6 volt system). Lock the adjusting screw, unclip the voltmeter and the job is complete. The figures I have given are for an average 12 volt unit, and will serve to keep yours working if you do not have access to the maker's figures. If you have the maker's figures, work to them.

Chapter 7 | The distributor and ignition

The principle of a coil ignition system (I am not going to delve back in the past to deal with magnetos here) is very simple and depends on two simple circuits. The first is the low tension (LT) side, which works at 12 volts. The low tension (LT) windings on the coil are fed from the ignition switch, and from there the circuit goes to earth on the distributor body via the contact breaker points which act as a switch—remember the feed-component-switch definition of circuit? While the points are closed and current is flowing in the low tension circuit (sometimes called the primary circuit) a high voltage is being built up in the secondary windings or high tension windings of the coil. When the points open, and the low tension current suddenly stops, the high voltage looks for a way to get back to earth. It finds it via the high tension (HT) lead to the centre of the distributor cap, the rotor, the plug lead (wire) and the points of the plug, across which it sparks. This time it is a feed-switch-component circuit, the feed being the low tension windings, the switch being the sudden cut off in the low tension current and the component being the sparking plug.

According to accredited research, ignition troubles account for the majority of roadside breakdowns. Most of these troubles come from the plugs, plug leads (wires) and contact breaker points, so if those of your car are at all old, renew the lot. They are not very expensive.

Little needs to be said about sparking plugs except to make sure you get the right type for your car. They are often referred to by their heat carrying capacity as 'hot' or 'cold' plugs, and the wrong sort in your engine can lead to misfiring. The type will be quoted in the car handbook,

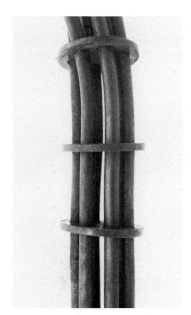

Above **Using drilled plastic spacers to keep the ignition harness tidy is less likely to lead to trouble than running them through a tube**

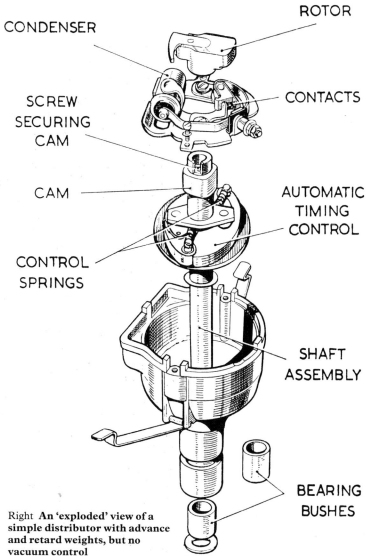

CONDENSER

ROTOR

SCREW
SECURING
CAM

CONTACTS

CAM

AUTOMATIC
TIMING
CONTROL

CONTROL
SPRINGS

SHAFT
ASSEMBLY

BEARING
BUSHES

Right **An 'exploded' view of a simple distributor with advance and retard weights, but no vacuum control**

and possibly on the chart you find with the plugs in an accessory shop. If not, write to the plug maker or the car maker and ask. Some older plugs are no longer produced, so you may have to fit a modern equivalent. Find out from the plug maker. The man in the accessory shop *might* know, but then again he might be guessing or quote a 'general' type of plug. In some cases fitting the wrong heat plug can prove expensive and it has been known to lead to burnt pistons.

Clean plugs either with a strip of emery cloth or a sand blasting cleaner, but it is false economy to use plugs for too long. 8000 to 10,000 miles is quite enough for the average plug. When they get old they tend to leak, and though they work well on a dry day they will probably give trouble when it's wet.

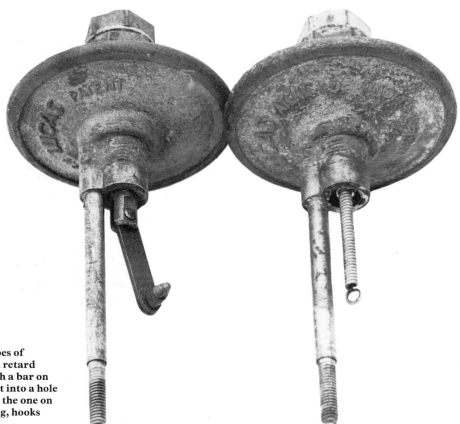

You may find two types of vacuum advance and retard controls. The one with a bar on the left hooks straight into a hole in the base plate, and the one on the right with a spring, hooks over a stud

The same goes for old plug leads (wires). These invariably leak (electrically) when they get damp, as you can prove by laying your hand on them with the engine running—you won't keep it there long. Most present day cars are fitted with suppressor plug leads to stop radio interference. These are fine when they are made up to length complete with terminals in a factory, but the conductor in them is a thin carbon strand which can be very awkward to fix to a terminal once the lead is cut. If you can't get a set of modern leads ready cut to size for your car I would advise using the older type of lead with a central stranded copper conductor together with separate suppressors. Not every accessory shop keeps this type of lead now, but it is worth shopping around. While you are about it, get some of the

This distributor looks rather a mess, but with a thorough clean, new points and a new condenser I found that it worked perfectly

split copper washers which are used at the ends of this type of lead. The old ones will probably be discoloured, even green, and though the spark will jump the corrosion, it burns the washer as it does so. If you can't get any washers, clean the old ones carefully.

Take a good look at the connectors, either screw-in or push-in on the chimneys of the distributor cap and the nose of the coil. They should be clean and smooth. If they are chipped or if there is any sign of a crack they will leak (electrically) to earth as soon as they get damp. You can't repair them, so renewal is the only cure. The same applies if there is any sign of cracking, or tracking, inside the distributor cap. Tracking is a thin burnt line where the high tension spark has been jumping along the plastic instead of going to the plug. If it has done it once, it will do it again.

Many cars built in the 1950s had the plug leads running neatly in a metal or cardboard composition tube. The metal

The bottom of the distributor has an offset D-drive. If you remove it to renew the bearings, make a note first of its position relative to the rotor arm slot at the top

ones can be cleaned, but the cardboard ones nearly always warp and often fall to pieces from the engine heat. A neat and good replacement (though not 'original') can be made from the hard type of plastic water piping you find in hardware or timber shops.

Coils do not often give trouble. though they are often suspected because you can't see what's happening inside. Check a coil with one of the multi-function diagnostic meters on the market, which will check its output, or you can make a rule of thumb check without one. To do this, take the high tension lead from the coil out of the top of the distributor cap, take the cap off, turn the engine so that the contact points are closed and switch the ignition on. Hold the end of the high tension lead about half an inch or so from a clean part of the engine—not near the carburettor or petrol pump—and flick the points open with a screwdriver. As you flick them open a high tension spark

Below **Check inside the distributor cap to see that the small carbon brush in the middle is not worn or stuck, and the inside of the cap is not damaged. On this one, the rotor had scored the cap (top) because the cap had not been put on straight**

Below **A common but sometimes baffling cause of misfiring is that the wires folded over the washer at the ends of the plug leads may have broken off**

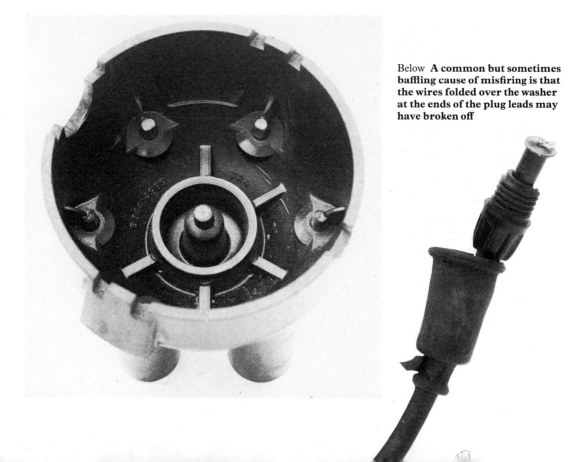

Accessibility was better on older cars. The coil was ideally placed on this Jaguar XK120 engine, but engine vibration wouldn't do it much good. Check for tight connections, at regular intervals

should jump from the end of the lead to the engine (all you are doing is working the switch manually). You will probably get a small spark at the points, but unless this is severe and the points are badly burned, it is nothing to worry about. If the distributor is not on the car for any reason, or you suspect the points or something else in the distributor, make the same check but this time take the low tension lead off the distributor as well and work the switch by touching it to a clean chassis earth (ground) point. If you get a good spark this time, but did not get one when you flicked the points open, the coil is probably all right but you have trouble in the distributor.

If you have one of the more modern coils the low tension terminals will probably be marked + and −, and so may some quite elderly coils. Others will have the terminals marked SW (for ignition switch) and CB (for contact breaker). You can use a coil on a negative or positive earth system provided you observe the correct polarity. If the

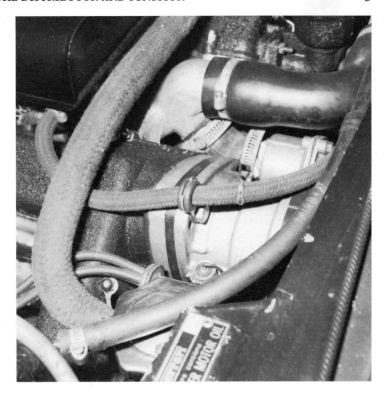

Supercars can be devils to work on. The Ferrari 246GT Dino's vee-6 engine has the distributor tucked in at one end of a cylinder head, almost obscured by body panels

terminals are marked SW and CB you will need to know what the polarity was on the car to which it was originally fitted. It was probably negative earth, but you must check this.

Some cars have ballasted coils. These are designed to work at about 9 volts for a 12 volt system, and there is a ballast resistor in circuit which is by-passed on starting to overload the coil and give the spark a boost. Sometimes the ballast resistor is a resistive lead from the ignition switch and sometimes it is a separate unit. There is a separate cable running from the same terminal on the coil to the starter solenoid. When the starter is operated, the cable from the solenoid by-passes the ballast resistor to send 12 volts across the coil.

The distributor will have at least one, and probably two methods of automatic timing advance to advance the timing of the ignition as the speed of the engine rises, or as the load on the engine changes.

In one type, the distributor cam is moved relative to the distributor drive spindle by a pair of centrifugal balance weights which move outwards as the speed increases. These are controlled by springs which may be of equal strength, or one spring may be stronger (with thicker wire) than the other. If this is so, the car workshop manual will probably call it a differential spring assembly. With this type, a variation is that one spring is under slight tension when the distributor is at rest, and the other is slack because there is a loop at its end instead of a round hole. The idea is to change the rate of advance as the engine speeds up and both springs come into action. It doesn't matter usually which spring fits to which balance weight, but the weights must be free, and both springs undamaged.

The second type of automatic advance is operated by the depression in the inlet manifold, often wrongly called the manifold vacuum. There is a 'vacuum' diaphragm unit mounted on the side of the distributor, and a thin pipe con-

The eight-cylinder distributor on the Chevrolet Corvette was at the back of the engine, almost but not quite shrouded by the air cleaner for the carburettor. The Delco wiper motor is very close to it. Note that the sensible owner has marked up the plug leads, so that he can re-assemble quickly when the distributor top has been off for attention

nects this to the inlet manifold. As the depression in the manifold changes with throttle opening and engine speed, the diaphragm moves and rotates the base plate of the distributor slightly so that the points are moved relative to the cam to advance or retard the timing. Check that the thin pipe is not blocked (blow through it) and that the diaphragm is not punctured. You can't get at the diaphragm, but if you blow into the end of the unit you ought not to be able to blow air through it. If you can, the diaphragm is leaking. Another possible fault is a corroded spring in the diaphragm housing. You can check this when the vacuum unit is off the distributor by pushing the connecting rod gently in and out. It should feel easy and smooth, not gritty and stiff. If you have to change the diaphragm unit make sure you get the correct type and rating. It is not sufficient to get one for the same model car, as sometimes these changed when the type of distributor was changed, and the change may be far from obvious. Nearly

On the Mercedes-Benz 300SL sports car, the wiper motor was in the corner of the engine bay, not hidden away under the dash, so removing and rebuilding should not be difficult. The coil was mounted nearby, not on the engine where it might suffer from heat and vibration

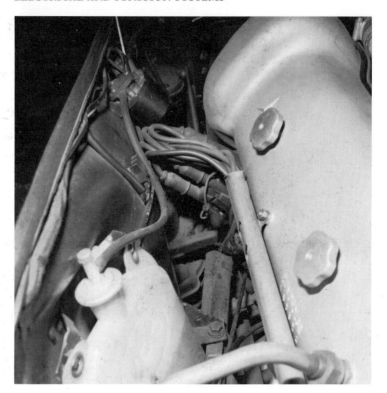

In some cars, the makers clearly assumed that their electrical components would never go wrong. Getting at the six-cylinder Bosch distributor in the Mercedes-Benz engine compartment is never going to be easy. Note, by the way, the neat way in which the HT leads are carefully tucked away into a tube along the side of the camshaft cover

all vacuum advance units are coded. In the case of a Lucas unit it will be a code—something like 3/24/12. The first figure gives the pressure depression in inches of mercury at which the unit starts to work against its spring. The second shows the depression at full travel and the third is the maximum advance in degrees of rotation of the base plate. Some vacuum units have a so-called 'micrometer' adjuster which isn't a micrometer at all but a knurled knob to adjust the setting manually. If you take this part to pieces, take care not to lose the ratchet and spring, for they are inclined to fly off when the knob is removed.

If the distributor shaft is slack in its bearings you will never be able to get consistent timing and never be able to set the points gap properly. On distributors for smaller cars the shaft runs in two bronze bearings, but on high performance cars the top bearing is sometimes a ball bearing.

To renew the bearings you must take off the drive mem-

Take heart, for this is not a post-war installation! The vee-12 Hispano Suiza, however, had *two* 12-cylinder distributors by Scintilla

ber at the bottom of the shaft. This is usually held by a pin, and may be a skew gear or a driving dog with offset 'dees'. In the case of the driving dog make a careful note of its position relative to the rotor arm before you knock the pin out or you might get the timing 180 degrees out when it is re-assembled.

The old bearings can be pressed out with a shouldered mandrel and new ones pressed in. There should be no need to ream bronze bushes as they are pre-sized to allow for closing as they are pressed in. You should soak them in engine oil for 24 hours before pressing them in, as they are designed to be oil retaining and get little or no lubrication in service.

When reassembled with its drive member the shaft should have a small end float for clearance—about 0.002 in. (0.05 mm). Sometimes this is controlled by a fibre washer under the dog and sometimes by a brass washer. If you get a new brass washer there will be three pips on it. Pin the driving dog or gear while it is pushed hard up against the washer and then give the end a smart blow with a mallet. This will squash the pips and give you the correct end float. I am assuming here that you have fitted a new shaft which has to be drilled for the pin. If you are re-using the old shaft you will have to use thin shim washers to get the end float.

If the points are badly burnt it may mean that the condenser (capacitor) is leaking. Its job is to absorb the sudden surge of current as the points open and close, and to reduce the sparking across the points. There isn't a satisfactory way to check it, so if you have doubts, renew it. On an old distributor you may have trouble getting one of the right size, but in this case you can fit it outside the distributor. Its centre lead goes to the low tension terminal and its body to chassis earth—usually the body of the distributor or a convenient nearby bolt. It is electrically better to fit it at the distributor rather than at the coil end of the cable.

Old rotor arms sometimes leak, and you can test this in a similar way to the method you used to test the coil. Go through the test in the same way but try to make the spark jump to earth through the brass top cap on the rotor arm. If it does, the arm is leaking and you need a new one. These cannot be repaired. It is also best to fit a new rotor arm if you fit a new distributor cap, as the brass part of the old one will have 'burnt in' to the brass studs in the old cap.

Before you refit the distributor, set the points gap to the figure in the book—0.012 to 0.014 in. (0.30 to 0.35 mm) is an average if you haven't got the figure. When refitting, follow the golden rule: set the distributor; set the engine; couple the two.

The manual will give the timing in terms of a number of degrees before top dead centre (TDC), usually on no. 1 cylinder—and remember that some makers number their cylinders on in-line engines from the back of the engine, not the front as is more usual. With vee engines or flat fours, make sure you know which is the manufacturer's no. 1. In most cases there will be a mark for timing either on the crankshaft pulley, or on the flywheel. Remember

Left **Rotor arms don't often give trouble, but sometimes they crack, and sometimes they leak HT current direct to electrical earth**

Below **To check the spark producing capabilities of the coil, flick open the points with the ignition switched on, and you should see a spark between this HT lead, and the engine's cylinder head.** *Not* **recommended if there are petrol fumes around!**

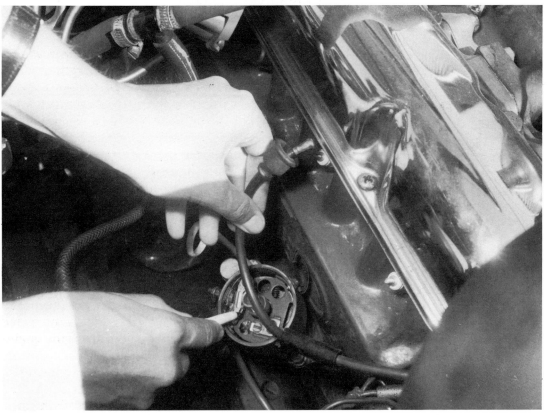

that this mark will come opposite its pointer every revolution of the crankshaft, but on a four-stroke engine only every other time will be firing position. You want the stroke when the cylinder is on compression, so check this by holding your thumb over the plug hole while someone turns the engine. You will feel the compressed gas hissing past your thumb. Make a double check that when the mark comes up to the pointer, both the valves on that cylinder are closed. If there are no timing marks, set the crankshaft just a shade before TDC. This will get the engine started, and you can fine tune it when it is running.

Now set the distributor by turning the shaft until the rotor arm is pointing to the stud inside the cap which feeds no. 1 cylinder, and the points are just about to open. Then feed the distributor into its hole in the engine. If it is an offset dog drive it should slot easily into place. If it is a skew gear, the shaft will turn as you feed it in, and give you a wrong setting. Note which way it turned. take it out and reset it by an equal amount the opposite way so that when it goes home the points are just about to open.

Final timing is left until the engine is running and warm. If you have timing marks the best way is to use a strobe lamp. Connect it according to the instructions, and shine it on the timing marks while the engine is running. The mark will appear to stand still and you can adjust the rotation of the distributor to get the timing spot on. You can also check that the automatic advance is working by speeding the engine up. If it is working, the mark will appear to move. Gentle acceleration checks the balance weight automatic advance, and if you snap the throttle open and the mark appears to move the vacuum advance is working. If you haven't got any timing marks, or haven't got a strobe lamp, set the distributor to give the fastest tick-over when the engine is warm and running just a *little* faster than normal tick-over, and then check it for performance on the road.

If you have a diagnostic meter, you can check the points gap by using the dwell setting. This gives an accurate measurement, far more accurate than you can get with feeler gauges.

Chapter 8 | Horns

Electric horns can be divided quite handily into two types, the high frequency 'beep-beep' type and the 'Windtone' type, though strictly speaking the name Windtone should be applied only to the ones made by Lucas, as they have a trade mark. Most of the musical two-note horns work on the same principle as a Windtone, and though the insides might look a little different they usually adjust in the same way.

Generally, horns last very well and don't give much trouble. When they do it can usually be put right by cleaning and adjusting. On the Lucas high frequency horn the adjuster has a click action. To set it, turn the screw anticlockwise till the horn just stops sounding, then screw it in again six clicks. This, within a couple of clicks or so either way, will be its best setting.

Do not alter the two coil securing screws or you will be in trouble and have to take the whole horn to pieces. Sometimes the horn will come to pieces after you undo a ring of screws, but more often you will find it is riveted and you will have to drill out the rivets and replace them with bolts and nuts. Inside you will find coils and a diaphragm vibrator. If the horn is so old and ill-treated that the insides are rusty, throw it away and get another unless it is a really early one and quite rare, in which case do your best to clean it up and puzzle out how best to set the vibrator so that it sounds well when you are within the range of adjustment given by the adjusting screw. Details differ, but you can spend an interesting afternoon, or two, puzzling it out and irritating the neighbours. . . . If you want to take off the heavy rim of a Lucas horn to get it re-chromium plated, if it was originally plated, it will usually come off without

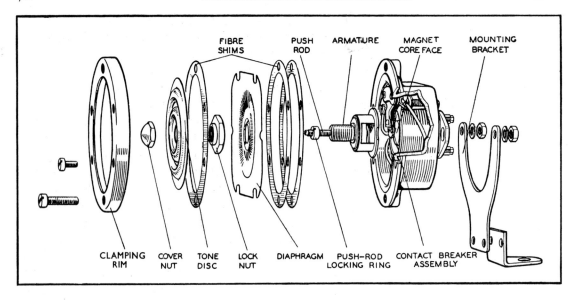

The components of the popular Lucas HF 1234 high frequency horn

disturbing the rest of the innards. If it was originally painted you might find that it is riveted and the same rivets hold other parts of the horn together, so take things apart carefully and expect a few parts to drop out on the floor. This type of horn is not very complicated, and usually with a bit of fiddling you can get it to work well, even if you don't know the factory settings. One of the best ways of making the final adjustments is to sound it with an ammeter in circuit. If it is working correctly, a 12 volt horn should not take more than 4 to 4.5 amps. A 6 volt horn will take more, depending on its power, but if it takes something excessive to work it, like 10 amps, it is way out of adjustment.

The old Klaxon-style ah-oooh-gar type of horn has a small electric motor in it, sometimes with a rotary sounding device, and sometimes with a cam which rotates and knocks up against a diaphragm to make the sound. In either case, the way it works is fairly obvious once you see inside. Poor operation is usually the result of worn carbon brushes in the motor, and as it is most doubtful that you will get the correct replacements you will have to search round various service agents for small motors, (model or hobby shops may be helpful) to find the nearest you can get, and you may possibly have to file them down to fit. It is a fiddly business, but quite satisfying once you get the thing working and sounding out well again.

Windtone horns come in pairs and are marked H and L, usually cast on the inside of the trumpet, to denote high or low pitch. The two pitches are a musical major third apart (unless you happen to find a pair of the (non-Lucas) raucous, dissonant type which were once on the market and which were tuned a semi-tone sharp on a major third to give a real camion-shifting discord. In either case you should have a pair of horns, one high and one low. Where only one was fitted, for economy (or penny-pinching, whichever way you look at it) reasons, it was generally the high pitch one which was retained. Under the domed cover is a vibrator with a pair of contact points which get dirty in time and affect the clarity of the tone. If these are badly burnt, the horn has been out of adjustment for a long time. You can get new points at some Lucas agents, though some staff will tell you they are not available which, in my experience, merely means 'not in stock'.

More expensive, but better quality, is the Lucas HF 1746 horn

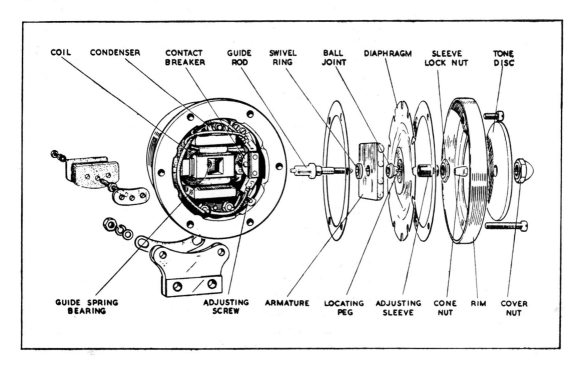

If the points are reasonable you can clean them with emery cloth, and reset them. Altering the points gap will not affect the tone but will affect the clarity and the current consumption. As a starting point for setting, slacken the locknut and turn the adjusting screw until the horn just fails to sound. Then turn it the opposite way half a turn and lock it. Make the final check with an ammeter in circuit. A Windtone horn should not take more than 8.5 amps to give a good loud note. If it does, either you have not cleaned the points properly, or they are not meeting properly, or the spring controlling one of them is cracked or tired.

A current of 8.5 amps, or 17 amps if you have a pair of horns, is far too high for the average steering wheel horn push, and will quickly burn it, so the horns have to be operated via a relay. This is simply an electrical switch. The terminals for the switch contacts inside the relay are connected in the feed to the horns, and the feed from the horn push operates the relay switch.

Usually, the horn push circuit is the feed-component-switch-earth type so that only one horn wire has to come up the steering column, the other side of the horn push being taken to chassis earth via the column. This means that the feed for the push circuit goes to one of the low current terminals on the relay. The wire from the other low-current terminal goes to the push button.

Below left **It is not always easy to tell from the outside what the quality of a horn is like. This is the inside of a cheap, un-named one**

Below right **The inside of a good quality horn, such as this Bosch, is very different and accounts for the higher price**

**Earlier Lucas Windtone horns
could be taken apart by undoing
nuts and bolts, but to get at the
diaphragm on later models (left)
six rivets have to be drilled out**

If you are fitting Windtones in place of a single high frequency horn which did not have a relay, the low-current
part of the relay takes the place of the original horn. You
have to take a second feed from the junction box to carry
the higher current for the Windtones to one of the high-
current terminals on the relay.

Keep the idea of the simple circuit in mind, and you
won't go far wrong. The terminals on the relay will be
marked with letters—A, B, and so on—so you will have
to refer either to the leaflet that should have been supplied
with it in the box, or to the wiring diagram of a vehicle
which uses an identical relay, to sort out which are the low-
current ones and which are the high-current ones. Sometimes, for a pair of Windtones or similar high-current
horns, the relay has six terminals, two for the low current
to operate it and a pair each for the horns to avoid it having
to carry 17 amps through one pair of contacts. So long as
you can identify the terminals, any relay of the right voltage will do the job.

The same principle applies if you want to use a relay
to operate any high-current component such as a 'flame-
thrower' spot or fog lamp or electric window winders.

Remember that no horn will sound properly if its
mounting bolts are not tight even though it may be
mounted through a spring steel blade as are many heavy
Windtones, particularly the sort with long straight trum-
pets. If you are making the adjustments off the car, clamp
the horn bracket firmly in a heavy vice.

Chapter 9 | SU electric fuel pumps

Over the years, SU electric fuel pumps have varied in details, mainly in the layout of the valves, and some are doubles, two horizontally opposed units working on a single central body to double the rate of flow, but despite these differences they all work on the same principle and they are all very similar to overhaul.

Trouble usually comes from sticking or worn contact points, sticking valves, dirty filters, or, more rarely, a diaphragm which has gone hard and lost its flexibility. There are differences in settings for different cars, so for details you should consult the manual or, if you are using a repair kit from SU, the leaflet which will cover all the types of pump for which the kit is suitable, in some cases on BL dealers' shelves, even though the particular model pump has been out of production for some time. In any case SU has always kept modern pumps in production which are direct replacements for older models, so you should never be entirely stuck for choice.

If you are dealing with a secondhand pump from an autojumble or the breaker's yard there will most likely be a nasty stale-smelling deposit of old petrol varnish inside the body. In some old manuals and books on car repair you might read that the way to get rid of this is to boil the parts in caustic soda solution followed by a dip in strong nitric acid, and a good rinse in boiling water.

I do not advise this. It gets rid of the old varnish very well, but it will most likely get rid of a sizeable portion of most modern SU pumps as well, on which the bodies are made from an aluminium based casting. The advice is a hang-over from the old days when the bodies of SU pumps were made from brass castings. In any case, caustic

The SU electric pump in its simplest form, with a single contact breaker

1. Outlet union.
2. Fibre washer (thick orange).
3. Spring clip.
4. Delivery valve disc.
5. Valve cage.
6. Fibre washer.
7. Suction valve disc.
8. Pump body.
9. Diaphragm assembly.
10. Armature guide rollers.
11. Retaining plate.
12. Filter.
13. Fibre washer (thick orange).
14. Filter plug.
15. Steel armature.
16. Push-rod.

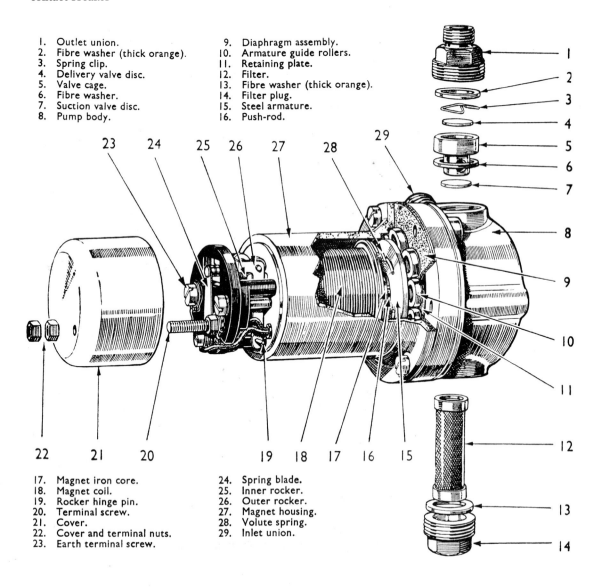

17. Magnet iron core.
18. Magnet coil.
19. Rocker hinge pin.
20. Terminal screw.
21. Cover.
22. Cover and terminal nuts.
23. Earth terminal screw.
24. Spring blade.
25. Inner rocker.
26. Outer rocker.
27. Magnet housing.
28. Volute spring.
29. Inlet union.

Some SU pumps have a double contact breaker (propped open here). It is important to see that both points meet squarely otherwise they will arc and burn quickly

soda and strong nitric acid are not very nice things to have around, so my advice is to ignore the old way.

If the deposit of varnish is light, scrubbing with methylated spirit or 'carb. cleaner' will shift it, and for getting inside the valve ports there are gum and varnish removing compounds available which do a good job safely, though please watch your eyes, and preferably wear goggles when you use them.

Start dismantling by taking off the plastic end cover. On the long terminal screw which holds it there are a number of washers, including a lead washer which squashes out when the nut is tightened, to make sure of a good electrical contact. This lead washer has to be cut away with a knife, and you must then use a new one, which will be supplied in the overhaul kit, when you put things together again. Take off the radio suppressor condenser if one is fitted, and the steel blade with one part of the contact points (it may be a single or a double set of points, depending on the model).

Now you can turn your attention to the other end and

undo the ring of screws holding the two parts of the body together, but mark the parts before you do so, so that you put them back in the same relative position. The number of screws may vary, and there may or may not be an earthing stud as well, depending on the model. There might also be an aluminium plate stamped with a number such as AUF200, which identifies the model of pump when you buy a repair kit. For the moment leave any filters or domed housings on the bottom part of the body. I will deal with those in a moment.

Take the two parts of the body apart carefully, over the bench, as there may be a number of brass rollers loose under the diaphragm. Collect and save them carefully, as they are not in the repair kit and not easy to obtain on their own. On later pumps you might find a shaped nylon armature guide in place of the brass rollers. Hook the two ends of this nylon guide free from the recess under the diaphragm, and lift it out. Treat it carefully; like the rollers it is sometimes difficult to obtain as a replacement part. Now you can unscrew the diaphragm and lift it out as an assembly together with its spring.

Going back now to the other end of the pump, take out the two screws which hold the black plastic rocker pedestal to the body, and lift it away complete with the rocker assembly. This is held in place by a hardened steel pin which can merely be pushed out. Take it out and store it carefully, as the pump will never work properly, or at least not for long, with a soft wire substitute. Don't try to take the core out of the magnet in the tubular part of the body. There is no need to take it out, and it can only be replaced or centred with special tools.

Your repair kit will contain a new rocker set, new contact blade, various washers, including the lead washer, and should also contain an assembly diagram showing the order in which all the parts fit. If it doesn't, or you are not using a kit, make a careful note of the order in which all the parts came off.

When you come to put the new rocker assembly on to the plastic pedestal, push the steel pin in position and then check that the centre toggle spring of the rocker assembly is above the spindle which carries the white rollers. It is

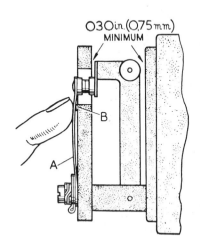

030 in. (0.75 mm) MINIMUM

When putting in new points, press the moving contact (A) against the small projection on the plastic base plate at point B, and measure the gap as shown. If necessary bend the contact blade slightly to get the right clearance

possible to get things inverted so that the action binds instead of working freely. Sometimes you might find that the
repair kit in its plastic bag has been handled a little harshly
in transit, and the rocker assembly has been pushed out
of true, so that it binds on the plastic. If so, straighten it
carefully with a small pair of pointed-nosed pliers. It is
quite weak and bendy until it is held by the diaphragm
rod, so take things gently.

The rest of the top assembly goes together in the reverse
order of taking it apart, but there are a couple of things
to keep in mind. The first is to remember to fit the lead
washer, with the coned face of the nut towards the lead
washer so that it is clamped like a pipe olive. The second
is that when you put in the two screws holding the plastic
pedestal to the body, one holds an earthing tag. The spring
washer goes between this tag and the pedestal, not on top
of the tag. It makes a better electrical contact that way
round. If there is a radio suppressor condenser, its tag takes
the place of the spring washer. Don't overtighten the
screws or you will crack the plastic, and hold the earthing
tag to stop it turning as there is a danger that it will be
pulled, and twist off. Leave the contact blade off for the
moment.

Go back to the other end of the body and fit the diaphragm, but before you do, fit the diaphragm spring in the
housing with its *smaller* end towards the diaphragm, thread
the small neoprene washer over the diaphragm spindle and
seat it in the recess at the end. Now is the time to push
the diaphragm spindle through the body and screw it into
the trunnion in the rocker assembly. As it goes home you
can check the action of the rocker by pushing the diaphragm spindle in and out against the spring. The rocker
should toggle over cleanly and without binding on anything. Screw in the spindle until the rocker will no longer
toggle over.

There are two types of rocker assembly, which I call an
early and a late type. If you have the late type (see diagram)
you have to fit the contact blade and check the rocker settings before you go any further. There are two stop fingers
on these later rockers, one to stop its action against the
pedestal and one to stop it against the body. Adjust the

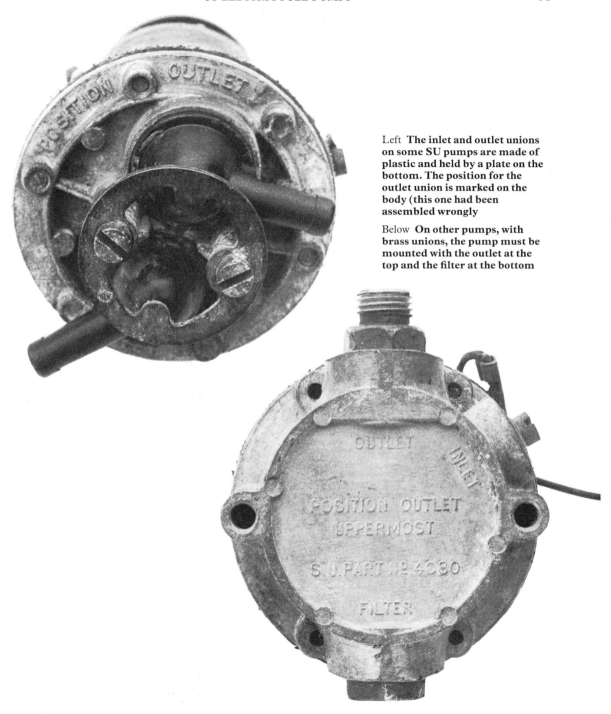

Left **The inlet and outlet unions on some SU pumps are made of plastic and held by a plate on the bottom. The position for the outlet union is marked on the body (this one had been assembled wrongly**

Below **On other pumps, with brass unions, the pump must be mounted with the outlet at the top and the filter at the bottom**

The fuel filters on electric pumps are often only visible when you have removed the body of the pump from the car. Check there is not a fluid blockage before you start blaming the electrics for non-delivery of fuel to the engine

top stop finger so that when the points are in contact, there is a gap of between 0.030 in. and 0.040 in. (0.75 mm and 1.0 mm) between the top of the pedestal and the underside of the contact blade. Then adjust the bottom stop finger to produce a gap between it and the top of the body of between 0.065 in. and 0.075 in. (1.65 mm and 1.90 mm). The fingers can be bent with a small pair of pliers to adjust them. When you have set the stop fingers, take the contact blade off again for the moment. The earlier type of rocker without the stop fingers does not have to be set, you adjust the points gap later if necessary. Now, in either case you are ready to move on to the next stage.

Put the brass rollers, if you have them, back under the diaphragm. If you have a nylon guide, you can leave it out for the moment.

Take care not to let any rollers fall out of position, hold the pump approximately horizontal, and push on the end of the diaphragm so that it can gently be unscrewed. Unscrew it a little at a time, as you press, then release, the pressure until you reach the point where the rocker will just toggle over when you push. Now carry on unscrewing

SU fuel pump terminals, and the points, should always be kept very clean. The cover should always be replaced, once the rebuild is over

till the nearest holes line up, and then for *a further four holes*. The diaphragm is now correctly set, and will not need any pre-stretching or flexing. Now push the diaphragm in and put a small fork wedge behind the rocker to hold the diaphragm in and prevent the brass rollers falling out while you attend to the other part of the body. If you have a nylon armature guide, set the diaphragm before you put it back in place.

With the main part of the pump reassembled, take the filters out of the bottom part of the body—they are under the unions on some types and under a screwed plug on others—and give them a good clean up in petrol. Take out the non-return valves, and if there is the slightest suspicion of their not seating or working properly, renew them. Test their seating by alternately blowing and sucking at the unions. Make sure they, or the new ones, go back the same way that they came out, or your pump will attempt to work in the reverse direction, and not do it very well.

On all but the smallest type of SU pump there are valve devices under domed covers, the purpose of which is to smooth the fuel flow so that it doesn't come out in a series of spurts. If the inside of the body was clean, it is best to leave these flow-smoothing devices alone, but if you are using a gum and varnish remover, you will have to dismantle these devices before you do. Take them apart carefully, and renew all the gaskets and neoprene washers—you can get them from an SU agent. He will probably tell you that the pump should be flow and pressure tested after these flow smoothing devices have been disturbed. Strictly speaking this is so, but if you are careful with the reassembly there is every chance that the pressure and flow will be as they were *before* you disturbed them. When assembling the flow smoothing device which has a tapered spring inside, you should hold the spring compressed while you tighten the cover screws. The only way to do this is to make up a small wire tool as shown in the diagram. You push it through the hole in the domed cover, thread the spring over it, followed by the spring end cap and hook the end cap on the tool so you can pull the spring back while you put the cover on and tighten the screws. Be careful not to damage the internal washers and diaphragms when you turn the tool to take it out again.

With all the valves in the body reassembled you can marry the two parts of the body—lining up the marks you made before you took them apart—and put the screws in finger tight. Remove the wedge from behind the rocker before you tighten the body screws.

Refit the contact blade, and position it is just above centre when it meets the contact on the rocker—the blade is slotted to allow adjustment—as shown in the diagram.

On the early type rockers without stop fingers, the last job to be done is to set the points gap. Before you do this, set the blade so that with the points open it makes contact with the small ridge on the pedestal—again, see diagram. Check the points setting indirectly by measuring the gap between the fibre rollers on the rocker and the body of the pump when the points are closed. It should be 0.030 in. (0.8 mm). If it isn't, bend the tip of the contact blade gently to adjust it, but make sure it still rests on the small ridge when the points are open.

The last job is to fit the end cover and the rubber band which seals it against moisture.

Chapter 10 | Windscreen wipers

Many cases of wipers failing to operate, overheating or operating sluggishly are due to faults in the linkage from the motor to the wiper arms, so always check this before you start removing and stripping down the motor.

Check the voltage at the motor before doing anything else, and if this is below 11.5 volts for a 12 volt system (or 5.75 volts for a 6 volt system), find the cause, which probably will be a bad contact on one of the cables or corroded points in the switch, and put that right before going any further.

Assuming the voltage is all right, disconnect the motor from the drive. With mechanical strip or rod linkages, the method is usually obvious, but with the type of motor which drives a tubular rack you have to take the top off the motor gearbox and disconnect the end of the inner rack from the 'push-pull' link, usually termed the cross shaft. On some motors, notably some Lucas DR and DL models, the dome on the gearbox cover is separate from the cover itself. This dome contains the setting pip for the limit switch. Scribe a line across the dome and the cover so that the dome can be put back in the same position, otherwise the wipers will probably stop halfway across the screen instead of to one side.

The outer case of the rack comes off after you undo the knurled (or sometimes hexagon) nut, and the method of unhooking the inner rack is simple to understand, though it differs on different makes and models.

Now for checking the current consumption. The wiper may be single speed, two speed, self limiting (which means that it stops at the edge of the screen when you switch off), self parking (parks down below the edge of the screen when

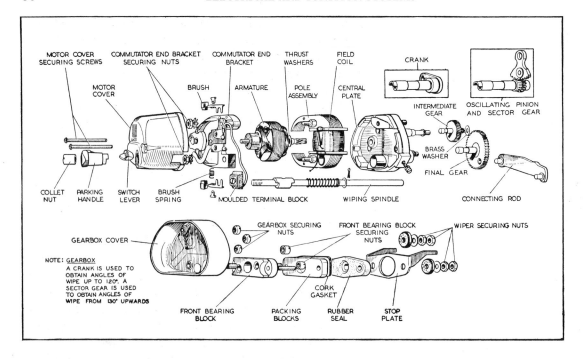

All the component parts of the Lucas FW2 screen-mounted wiper, which was popular on open sports cars in the 1950s

you switch off) or might even have a single flick-wipe facility. There may be four or five wires going to it, ending in a multi-plug connector. There will probably be a convenient bullet-type connecting block in the cable line near the wiper where one can disconnect the cables and test the current consumption without worrying about possible faults in the switch mechanism. If not, ask your local garage or electrical agent if he can supply you with a new multi plug and cable. Most can, and it's usually not very expensive.

With the bullet connectors undone, or your substitute plug and cable plugged into the motor—or if you've got only a simple wiper with two leads coming from it, with two slave leads in their place—you can consult the car's wiring diagram to see which of the leads goes to earth and which are the feed leads for the various functions. In a few cases you might find there are *two* earth leads.

Make up a couple of leads with crocodile clips at each end (this is always a useful special tool). Use one to connect the earth leads or leads to a clean part of the chassis and use the other to feed current straight from the battery, via an ammeter, to each of the feeds in turn. The motor should then operate with its various functions.

An important point to watch out for on some installations, is the sequence of the circuit—remember our two types of simple circuit? If, when you trace out the wiring diagram you find that there are two earth leads from the motor, the circuit is probably: feed, motor, switch, earth, so connect only one earth lead to chassis earth at a time or you might try to get two functions working at once which may not do the motor or your ammeter a great deal of good. For many fairly modern Lucas motors your Lucas agent can sell you a test plug and leads with four leads coloured blue, yellow, white and red. The normal test sequence is: feed to red, blue to earth for normal running; feed to yellow plus blue to earth for high speed running on two speed wipers; and feed to red plus white to earth for self parking wipers, but it may differ for different models, so ask the Lucas agent (or Bosch or AC Delco or Ducellier or whoever) when you buy the test plug.

The older CW model screen-mounted wipers were similar to the FW. Some had a sector and gear final drive, but others had a crank pin. Always mark the drives before you take them apart

For all these tests the current should not be more than 3.5 to 4 amps in most cases; always check the figure with the agent or with a specification handbook. If the motor is sluggish, usually with a high current consumption, or

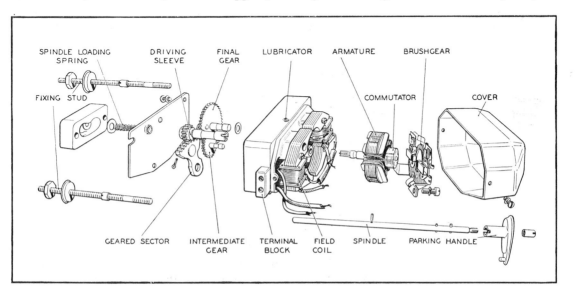

SPINDLE LOADING SPRING   DRIVING SLEEVE   FINAL GEAR   LUBRICATOR   ARMATURE   BRUSHGEAR

FIXING STUD   COMMUTATOR   COVER

GEARED SECTOR   INTERMEDIATE GEAR   TERMINAL BLOCK   FIELD COIL   SPINDLE   PARKING HANDLE

if it won't operate at all, it needs stripping down for over-haul. If it passes the tests, look elsewhere for the trouble—either in the switch or in the rack mechanism.

If you decide the motor needs stripping down for over-haul, take it apart carefully and watch out for any shims which might be used to control end play on any of the moving parts. Many wipers come apart after through-bolts are undone, or by undoing separate bolts under one of the end covers. On canister-type motors where there does not appear to be any method of undoing things, try unscrewing the body of the canister itself with a strap spanner.

If the motor has a gearbox built into it, this part will be packed with a high melting point grease. This is usually a very sticky grease, so try not to spread it into the electrical part of the motor. Most of it can be scooped out with a wooden paddle or spatula. Next, disconnect the electrical part from the gearbox and wash out the gearbox with a degreaser. I would advise against using petrol for this as the fumes can hang around long after you think they are

Inside the gearbox of a Lucas DR wiper motor. The parking switch which is operated by the sliding crosshead is adjustable by turning the knurled knob on the outside. A common trouble is that the cable from this switch chafes where it comes out of the body

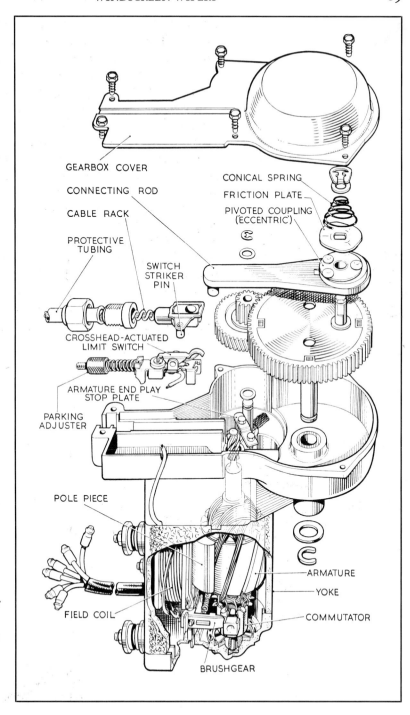

GEARBOX COVER

CONNECTING ROD

CABLE RACK

PROTECTIVE
TUBING

SWITCH
STRIKER
PIN

CROSSHEAD-ACTUATED
LIMIT SWITCH

ARMATURE END PLAY
STOP PLATE

PARKING
ADJUSTER

POLE PIECE

FIELD COIL

BRUSHGEAR

CONICAL SPRING

FRICTION PLATE

PIVOTED COUPLING
(ECCENTRIC)

ARMATURE

YOKE

COMMUTATOR

For larger screens and bigger wipers, Lucas introduced a more powerful motor with a spur gear drive instead of a worm and wheel. This meant the armature had to be mounted below the gearbox instead of at the side, but in most other aspects the motors are similar

Getting at this Delco wiper motor
for the 1968 model Corvette will
not be easy. It will probably come
out without moving the engine,
but there really isn't much
clearance from the distributor

dispersed, and as most motors spark at the commutator
there could be an explosion if there are any fumes left
inside.

When you are taking the gearbox apart, keep a piece of
rag over things if you have to take off any circlips. Often
these circlips have no ears on them, so you have to lever
them off with a screwdriver. Without a piece of rag to absorb them they are likely to fly off suddenly, and you will
lose them on the floor. It is unlikely that the gears will be
worn to any extent, but some of the bearings may show
signs of sloppiness when you clean all the grease out. Most
wiper motors will continue to work with a surprising
amount of slop in the bearings, but these are likely to be
noisy and difficult to suppress for radio interference. Some
agents, but not all, stock replacement bearings for wiper
motors. It depends whether they repair motors on the
premises, or send them away. It is most unlikely that you

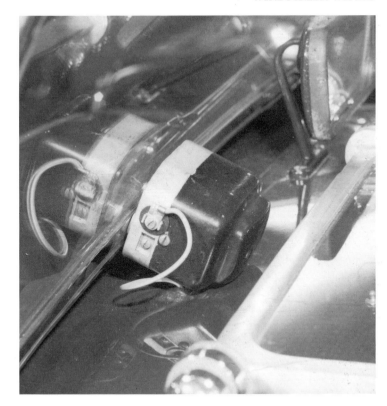

Below **On the Lotus Elan of the 1960s, the electric motor for the cooling fan was mounted rather precariously like this, behind the radiator block. You can see how errant wires might be savaged by the rotating fan blades**

Above **Some traditional sports cars, built in Europe, retained this sort of windscreen wiper motor, fixed directly to the windscreen, until the 1950s. One of the biggest problems facing a restorer is that such a motor may often have suffered a drenching, when rained on**

will find any parts for a motor in a normal garage, except perhaps for carbon brushes.

The brushes may be small strips of carbon held in holders by a wire spring. They may have leads fixed to them or they may be clamped in a rocking or pivotted arm. With the latter variety, the agent will tell you they have to be renewed as an assembly, which is only convenient if he has them in stock. For some older wipers these assemblies are difficult to obtain, but often you can get out of trouble by buying the nearest size of loose brush, and then file and sandpaper it down to size. They can be rubbed down quite easily, but use a very fine file as they are brittle; a coarse file will crack or chip them. They are usually held in the arms by folded tags.

It helps to bed the new brushes against the curve of the commutator. Some sources tell you to do this by wrapping a piece of glass paper round the commutator while the brushes are in place, but I find it most fiddling to try this when the commutator is in place. There isn't enough room. However, the amount of bedding-in is quite small and you can do it successfully with the parts dismantled. You may not get it perfect, but it will make better contact than a flat ended brush.

Clean the commutator with glasspaper and check its freedom of rotation and its end float. Quite often the end float is controlled by a screw and locknut, but on some motors there is a screw by itself which stays in place because it is a tight fit in the housing. Once moved, it often becomes loose, and is best replaced with a longer screw and a locknut. In other cases you may find the end float is controlled by small shim washers on the shaft. Makers quote an end float in thousandths of an inch, but it is difficult to measure this without a dial gauge, so set it so that the armature is perfectly free without actually rattling—an end float of between 0.005 in, and 0.008 in. (0.13 mm and 0.20 mm) is about right if you can measure, or judge it.

Some wiper motors have a thermostatic circuit breaker which cuts the current to the motor if it gets too hot. These are self-setting, and make contact again when the motor cools down—a fact which often causes frustration because the wiper refuses to work, then works perfectly again when you try it after a 10 minute delay.

The reason for the motor overheating is probably that there is a stiff rack or wheelbox where the arms fit, but it might—on some types of wiper motor such as some AC Delco models—be because the self aligning bearings have not re-aligned themselves after being knocked out of adjustment. In most cases they can be re-aligned by the simple method of thumping gently but firmly round the motor with a rubber or wooden mallet until the armature is seen to spin quite freely again.

If you think the fault lies in the thermostatic safety switch, you can test it by putting the motor under 'stall' conditions—by applying current to it while the armature is held stationary. The thermostatic switch should take at least half a minute to cut out. In cold weather it might take up to a quarter of an hour to operate on a heavy-duty motor, but generally it will cut out after a maximum of

Left **A 1950s type Bosch
installation in the Mercedes-Benz
300SL 'gullwing' sports car,
showing the windscreen wiper
motor, clearly wired, mounted on
the bulkhead where it was easy to
get at**

Right **In this case, the wiper
motor is ideally placed, and you
might be able to work on it, or
adjust it, without taking it out of
the car**

Right **With the end cover
removed, the brushes on this
windscreen wiper are easily
inspected, and are quite simple to
renew**

Above **The contact pad on the
parking switch of the wiper
motor may have worn because of
arcing, but it can easily be
cleaned up, by using fine glass
paper**

Above **Brushes for wiper motors
usually come in pairs. The fibre
retaining plate was not always
fitted to early models, but can
usually be added at an overhaul.
Its main purpose is to hold the
brushes securely in place**

five minutes. Make sure there *is* a thermostatic switch built
in before you try this test.

Your local agent will probably tell you that you must
replace the motor if the thermostatic switch is faulty,
because they are not available as a separate part and can't
be repaired. He is probably right on the first count, but
I quote (with permission) from the Lucas training manual:
Special factory equipment is used in production for assembling the circuit breaker to the motor yoke. This component is therefore not normally regarded as suitable for individual replacement. However, if replacement of the complete motor is impractical, the circuit breaker may be
removed from the yoke and resetting attempted as des-
cribed below. In this event, care must be taken on reassembly to see that the circuit breaker is rigidly secured to the
yoke.

The circuit breaker cannot be reset *in situ*. Therefore
remove it from the motor yoke and, with a suitable tool,
bend the moving contact blade carrier (a ribbed steel strip)
at the necked point, using the projections provided for this
purpose. Refit the circuit breaker to the yoke and retest.

The same, or similar, advice applies to most makes and,
indeed, to other electrical parts. The reason agents are

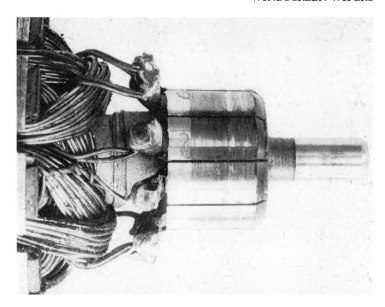

Left **A corroded wiper commutator can usually be cleaned up by using fine glass paper, but if a ridge is present, it should be skimmed lightly on a lathe. Always be sure to clean out the slots between the segments, to preserve the ideal electrical circuitry**

Below **Exploded view of a GM wiper motor, which is so typical of that company's post-war products**

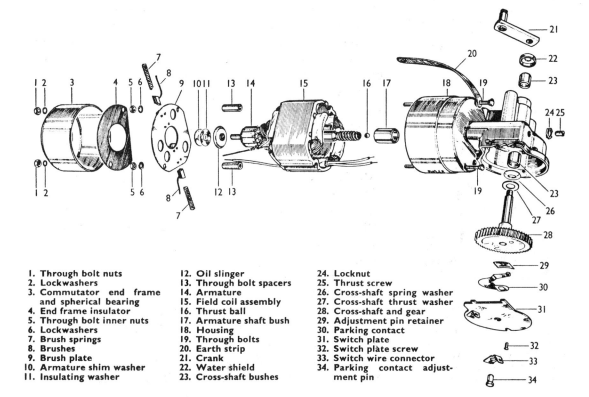

1. Through bolt nuts
2. Lockwashers
3. Commutator end frame and spherical bearing
4. End frame insulator
5. Through bolt inner nuts
6. Lockwashers
7. Brush springs
8. Brushes
9. Brush plate
10. Armature shim washer
11. Insulating washer
12. Oil slinger
13. Through bolt spacers
14. Armature
15. Field coil assembly
16. Thrust ball
17. Armature shaft bush
18. Housing
19. Through bolts
20. Earth strip
21. Crank
22. Water shield
23. Cross-shaft bushes
24. Locknut
25. Thrust screw
26. Cross-shaft spring washer
27. Cross-shaft thrust washer
28. Cross-shaft and gear
29. Adjustment pin retainer
30. Parking contact
31. Switch plate
32. Switch plate screw
33. Switch wire connector
34. Parking contact adjustment pin

unwilling to repair, or the maker does not supply a part separately is, in many cases, because the part is rivetted into position and set by automatic machinery on the production line. Taking it out, repairing it, resetting it, replacing it and testing it by hand is likely to take a long time, and even if there were a high chance of success the labour and parts cost could easily exceed the cost of a new or exchange unit. It can be frustrating, but the home restorer can often save quite a lot of money by adjusting non-adjustable parts or perhaps cannibalising another non-working component to obtain a part.

On almost all motors that drive through a rack there is some means of adjusting the setting position of the wiper arms when they are switched off. On some, part of the casing contains a striker for operating a trip to reverse the direction of the motor briefly, so that instead of driving the arms across the screen at the end of the stroke on which

This wiper motor has suffered from the ingress of water, and ruined the grease, which has emulsified. However, all was not lost, as there was only surface rusting of parts of the gears themselves

Right **On this Lucas wiper motor
the brass blade switch was
corroded, but when cleaned up,
the motor was almost as good as
new**

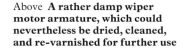

Above **A rather damp wiper
motor armature, which could
nevertheless be dried, cleaned,
and re-varnished for further use**

you switch off, it takes the arms down clear of the screen.
Alternatively, the motor takes the arms to one side of the
screen before it stops. Putting the switch on the dash or
steering column to 'Off' in these cases does not cut current
from the motor, it directs the current to a circuit inside
the motor which includes a limit switch. This switch operates only when the arms reach the desired position.

If it shuts off with the arms in any other position, you
must adjust the setting of the limit switch. In some cases
there is a knurled knob on the outside of the motor to adjust
the setting. In other cases, a part of the motor casing has
to be slackened and turned, and in yet more cases the
adjustment can be made only when a cover plate is taken
off the motor. There have been so many different designs
from a variety of makers over the last 30 years or so that
it is quite impossible to go through them here, even if I
had setting details for them all. Really, you must watch
carefully what happens, find the limit switch and work out
how to adjust it.

A completely different sort of motor is the type which
was designed to fit on the top flange of the windscreen in

the days when windscreens opened with a hinge at the top. These are all basically pre-war designs, but were used long after the war on open sports cars such as T-Series MGs.

Usually they are not self-parking, or even self-setting. The arm spindle usually protrudes out of the back of the motor and has a handle on it. It can be turned quite independently of the motor for parking the arm, by pulling the handle out. Often, in the park position, the end of the handle engages with the end of the switch lever to save it being operated accidentally.

These motors are quite simple to strip and repair, but take care to mark the teeth on all the gears where they engage (if they are not already marked with centre-pops) so that you put them back in the same engagement. Otherwise you will have trouble getting the spindle positioned so that it wipes an arc evenly to either side of the vertical position.

Troubles are usually confined to three faults: bending or breaking of one of the pins through the arm spindle, which act as dogs to engage the spindle with the motor; corrosion of the arm spindle where it passes through the windscreen flange; and worn brushes or a dirty commutator.

The commutator can be cleaned with glass paper, and you may be lucky enough to find new brushes. If not, you can usually find some which will file down to fit. If a replacement for a corroded spindle cannot be found, cannibalise another old motor. The pins in the spindle are hardened, and in the days when gramophones used steel needles these were an excellent source of replacements. Nowadays, try your local DIY shop for thin masonry nails or hardened picture-hanging pins. To cut these hardened pins to length, nick them with a fine file, then snap them with two pairs of pliers. If you take the field coils and pole pieces off this type of motor, leave the fixing screws loose until you have put the armature back in place. The holes in the pole pieces are made large enough to adjust them until the armature spins freely between them.

All wiper motors with gears should have the gear compartment packed with a high melting point grease. Ordinary chassis grease is useless, for it melts and runs all over the electrics.

Chapter 11 | Trafficators, heaters, screenwashers, switches and things

Trafficators

Semaphore trafficators have been relegated almost to the same quaint era as acetylene lamps by most motorists, but if you are restoring a car fitted with them it is nice to have them working properly. Electrically they are robust and seldom burn out. Most of the troubles are centred in the mechanical link between the arm and the operating plunger.

In electrical principle they are simple solenoids, with the plunger pulling down on a hinge link to raise the arm. Provided they are not jamming in their housings, arms fail to lift when current is applied to the solenoid due to corrosion, stiffness from lack of lubrication or damage to the locking plate. The locking plate's job is to stop the trafficator arm from bouncing when it is down. If you have ever tried to lift the arm of a trafficator you will know that it resists at first, then comes free with a click. Do this too many times—and most trafficators have had it done to them far too many times—and the locking plate gets bent.

The action of the locking plate is very simple, as you will see when you examine it. When the arm is down, the plate toggles over the centre so that it resists the lifting of the arm but offers no resistance to being pulled down by the solenoid plunger. When there is no current to the solenoid you should free the locking plate by pushing down on the top of it with a screwdriver or similar tool before you try to lift the arm. If you do this a few times and watch the action of the arm at its hinge you will be able to see if anything has been bent and is stopping the arm from coming up easily.

On some trafficators the amber plastic part may have

been detached, so you can hunt at autojumbles for another one if it is broken. On other types the amber plastic is held to the hinge of the arm by a rivet so that if it has been broken you will have to find another trafficator with an undamaged arm. Picking up on the end of the solenoid winding, or on the terminal feeding it, is a wire which carries current to the festoon bulb in the plastic part of the arm. Sometimes there is also an earth wire running back to the metal body, but on other models earthing is through the metal top of the arm. Whichever method of earthing is used, it must make proper contact both with the bulb and the body of the trafficator, and the body of the trafficator must make good earth contact, with the body of the car. Bad earthing is a common reason for trafficators failing to work.

Straightening any bent links, cleaning and lubricating, usually works wonders with old trafficators. Be sparing with the lubrication. If someone before you has smothered everything in oil in an attempt to get it all to work you may have to strip the mechanism to clean it, but do this only as a last resort. First, try cleaning with methylated spirit and a brush or with an aerosol of carbon tetrachloride. Old oil on the solenoid plunger is a frequent cause of sticking. When you relubricate, put just a touch of machine oil on the catch pin of the locking plate, and just a trace of high melting point grease on the link at the top of the plunger.

Some trafficators are placed in their own housings, but most were mounted in a slot in the door pillar or just behind it. The body of the trafficator has elongated holes to enable you to position it where the arm will be free to rise in the slot. When the arm drops it rests against a small buffer plate, usually with a rubber button in it. This plate often becomes bent and the arm either pokes out from the body of the car or drops back so that it leaves a gap. You should set the buffer plate by bending it with a pair of pliers after the trafficator is mounted on the car so that the chromium plated top of the arm is flush with the edge of the car's body.

If you are repairing a semaphore type trafficator, push down on the arm locking plate with a small screwdriver before you try to lift the arm or you will be likely to bend the small lifting plate

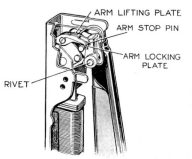

ARM LIFTING PLATE
ARM STOP PIN
ARM LOCKING PLATE
RIVET

Heater motors

Electric motors for heater blowers are usually classed as 'sealed units', and it is doubtful if you will find anyone stocking parts for them. Probably this is because of labour charges again, because they are very simple to repair if they have not burnt out.

The hardest part of the repair is usually to get the motor out of the heater, and to get the fan or squirrel cage rotor off the shaft. Sometimes these are held to the shaft by grub screws, but more often they are held by a nut tightened over a split collet, rather like a small drill chuck. The idea is the motor, should it give trouble, can easily be replaced as a unit, but it seldom works out that way. Most heater motors are used in the winter when they draw in moist, often salt-laden air, and then stand idle most of the summer, so that corrosion can weld the fan securely to the

Most heater motors are quite simple in construction and can be taken apart for cleaning and putting in new brushes, even though they were never intended to be repaired. Be sure to keep all the spacers and springs in order, and do not disturb any spherical bearings if you can help it, because they are put in the body with a special press and are very difficult to replace by hand

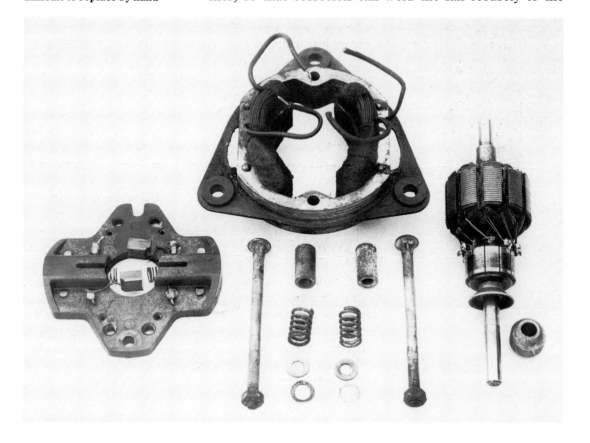

Many cars were fitted with push-pull switches. Most of them can be taken apart to clean the contacts if they give trouble, but on the type which turn as well as pull and push, such as this lighting switch, the small nut on the end of the shaft was usually locked with solder to stop it working loose

Many panel warning lamps use low voltage bulbs and have a resistance built into the body. If this becomes damaged it can be replaced with an ordinary tubular resistor such as used in radios

motor shaft. The only answer I know is to soak the offending part liberally in a freeing agent such as WD-40 or Plus Gas and if necessary apply a little heat from a small butane torch. *Don't* get things too hot or you will damage the shellac or plastic insulation of the motor windings.

Assuming you have managed to get the motor out of the heater and the fan off the shaft, the motor itself comes apart quite easily in the majority of cases. Usually there are long through bolts similar to those used in a starter or dynamo. The thing to watch for here is that on many motors there may be quite a number of collars, springs and distance pieces threaded on these through bolts, to position the various components of the motor. If you just pull the bolts out without thinking, the motor collapses in a heap of parts on the bench and can be worse than a Chinese puzzle to put together again. As you take each bolt out, thread a length of stout wire in its place so that you can dismantle the motor gently to see where everything fits. Be particularly careful on some motors which have spherical self-aligning bearings. Often these are held in the casing of the motor by leaf springs with fingers. The bearings pull out quite easily, but they are a devil of a job to get back in without unrivetting the leaf springs.

You may have to unsolder some of the wires to get the brush holder out, and the carbon brushes will probably be held by tags bent over at the end of the brush tube. These tags are sometimes brittle and snap off easily. Though you may have difficulty in finding replacement brushes labelled for heater motors, they are usually plain rectangular brushes and you ought to be able to find some others which can be modified to fit. Alternatively look in another old heater motor made by the same maker. I have found that although the motors differ widely in size and fixing arrangements to suit different types of heater, the same carbon brushes were fitted to a wide range of models. Even if a secondhand motor does not fit your heater, the brushes may well do so.

The commutator can be cleaned with a petrol moistened rag or with fine glass paper. You will probably have to solder the leads of replacement brushes to terminals on the brush carrier plate, and it makes matters easier if you take

the plate out of the motor. This means unsoldering two more wires from the field coils as a rule, but these are often more easy to resolder with the carrier in position than are the brush leads. It depends on the type of motor, so study it carefully before you pull it apart. Some motors have a wire-wound resistance in one lead, so remember to replace it.

Above **Quite a few pre-war and early post-war cars used this simple type of dip switch where the blade flicked over from one terminal to the other.**

Below **When you take out a dash panel for rewiring it looks very daunting, but if you go about things in a logical order, and replace one wire at a time, much of the complexity disappears**

Screen washers

Screen washer motors are another example of a small motor which was never intended to be taken apart for repair but which can often be repaired quite easily. Few can be dismantled by undoing screws or bolts, for most have tags on the case bent over to hold the end plates in position, or may even be crimped all round the plate, but if the motor isn't working you have nothing to lose by trying to take it apart. Inside you will find the usual arrangement of

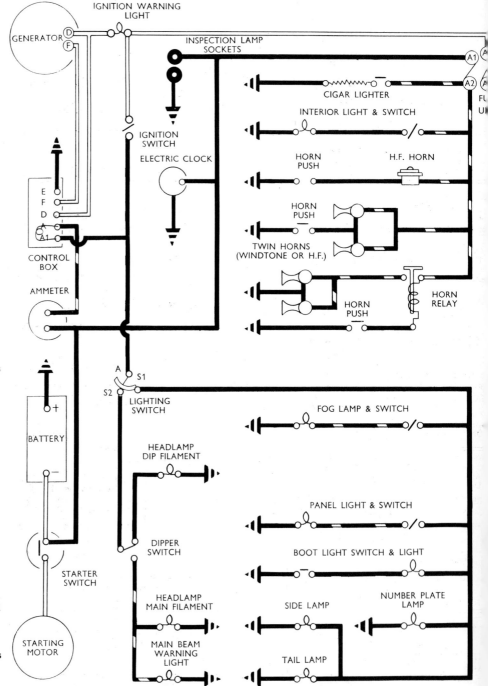

A typical circuit diagram of a car's wiring. Notice how all the circuits can be broken down into sections. These are, components which are not controlled by the ignition switch, components which are controlled by the ignition switch—which can again be split into groups—and the lighting circuits. Each of the groups will have a different coloured wiring system usually with 'tracer' colours to identify the cables to each component

Lucas
0122825809

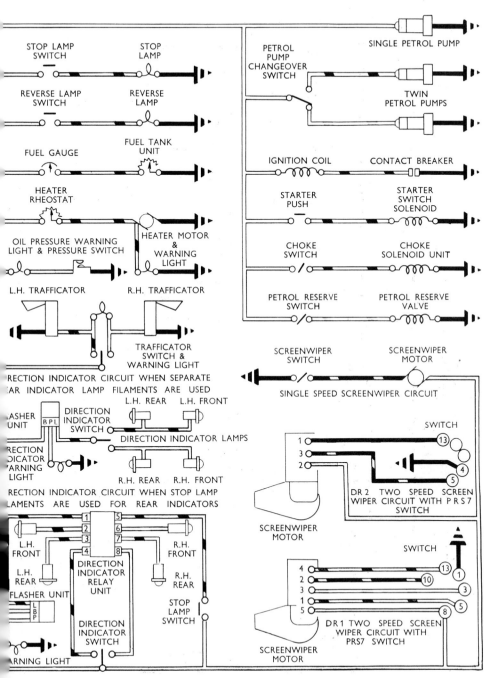

STOP LAMP SWITCH   STOP LAMP

REVERSE LAMP SWITCH   REVERSE LAMP

FUEL GAUGE   FUEL TANK UNIT

HEATER RHEOSTAT

OIL PRESSURE WARNING LIGHT & PRESSURE SWITCH

HEATER MOTOR & WARNING LIGHT

L.H. TRAFFICATOR   R.H. TRAFFICATOR

TRAFFICATOR SWITCH & WARNING LIGHT

DIRECTION INDICATOR CIRCUIT WHEN SEPARATE REAR INDICATOR LAMP FILAMENTS ARE USED

FLASHER UNIT

B P L

DIRECTION INDICATOR SWITCH

L.H. REAR   L.H. FRONT

DIRECTION INDICATOR LAMPS

DIRECTION INDICATOR WARNING LIGHT

R.H. REAR   R.H. FRONT

DIRECTION INDICATOR CIRCUIT WHEN STOP LAMP FILAMENTS ARE USED FOR REAR INDICATORS

L.H. FRONT

L.H. REAR

FLASHER UNIT

L B P

DIRECTION INDICATOR RELAY UNIT

DIRECTION INDICATOR SWITCH

R.H. FRONT

R.H. REAR

STOP LAMP SWITCH

WARNING LIGHT

SINGLE PETROL PUMP

PETROL PUMP CHANGEOVER SWITCH

TWIN PETROL PUMPS

IGNITION COIL   CONTACT BREAKER

STARTER PUSH   STARTER SWITCH SOLENOID

CHOKE SWITCH   CHOKE SOLENOID UNIT

PETROL RESERVE SWITCH   PETROL RESERVE VALVE

SCREENWIPER SWITCH   SCREENWIPER MOTOR

SINGLE SPEED SCREENWIPER CIRCUIT

SWITCH

1
3
2

13
4
5

DR 2 TWO SPEED SCREEN WIPER CIRCUIT WITH P R S 7 SWITCH

SCREENWIPER MOTOR

SWITCH

4
2
3
1
5

13   1
10
3
5
8

DR 1 TWO SPEED SCREEN WIPER CIRCUIT WITH PRS7 SWITCH

SCREENWIPER MOTOR

Right **On older cars, there was space to work on the wiring, but they were not always installed tidily. This, by the way, was an early type of screen wash, with motor in the top, and with a glass bottle**

Left **On some cars, there was no cover over the fuse block, which made the fuses rather vulnerable to damage by flying spanners, or by water and mud ingress. If you strip down, you *must* make a note of which wires fix to which terminals!**

How on earth can you hope to get at fuse boxes positioned like this on a Ferrari? Patience, and sticky fingers, all help!

commutator and brushes, but you might also find some nylon or similar plastic sleeving on the shaft, squashed against a bracket by the end plate. This is a seal to stop water and screen cleaning fluid from finding its way into the motor, and if you don't get it sealing properly again the repaired motor could have quite a short life.

Switches
Most switches that give trouble can be helped by squirting switch cleaner into the contacts, and working the switch back and forwards a few times. If you have difficulty in getting switch cleaner from a garage, try a shop that caters for electronics enthusiasts. If this fails you will have to take the switch apart and clean the contacts with fine glass paper. Some switches are simple, but some column mounted multi function switches that push, pull, lift and turn can be quite complicated inside, with the 'click' position for each function ensured by small coil springs. They are seldom made to be taken apart, and most of the compo-

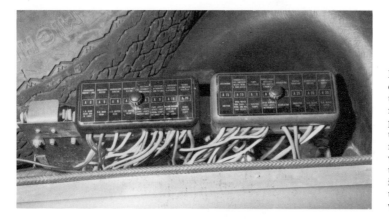

Below **Somewhere in there is the electric motor for a thermostatically-controlled radiator cooling fan. Access will probably be easier from the underside of the car. These motors not only suffer from vibration, but from corrosion due to salt flung up from the roads. It is amazing how much easier it is to restore the electrics of a car which lives in a dry climate**

Above **You don't always need a degree in languages to understand the electrical systems of European cars. This set of fuses in Magneti Marelli installations have plastic covers with Italian and English labelling**

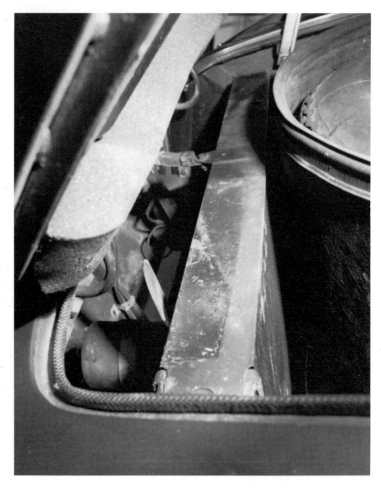

This type of terminal for pre-focus headlamp bulbs may have been crimped or soldered. This is production line crimping, not ideally done, for the wire should not have been exposed

nents are held by rivets or by folded tags. If you have to take one apart because you can't get a replacement, study it closely before you even attempt to unrivet or unbend any tags.

Later dash-mounted switches of the rocker type are usually renewable, and are so cheaply made from plastic that they are not worth working on, but most older switches can be taken apart and cleaned. Rotary dash mounted lighting switches can often be dismantled after a spring ring is taken off the back, but if the ignition key switch is built in as well, watch out for a small toggle on the back of it which may easily drop out and be lost when you take the back cover off.

On older cars the dash mounted warning lights often use low voltage bulbs and have a wire resistance wound round the lamp holder to cut the 12 volts down to the bulb voltage. These were made in the days before small 12 volt bulbs were generally available, and though garages seldom stock the older low voltage bulbs you can get them from most shops that sell torches or bicycle lamps. If the resistance is damaged you can replace it with a tubular resistor from a radio components shop. Most of the lamps take a 2.5 volt bulb, so for a 12 volt system you will need a 50 ohm resistor, and for a 6 volt system a 20 ohm. Normal radio resistors have a tolerance of plus or minus 15 per cent, and this is close enough for our purpose. There is no need to go to the trouble of finding close tolerance resistors.

Chapter 12 | **Trouble shooting**

It's all very well knowing how to strip down and repair faulty components, but if you don't know how to find and isolate the trouble, you never know which part of the circuit is at fault. You can spend many fruitless hours trying this and trying that, all to no avail.

This is where your meter and your knowledge of the basic simple circuit come in. Let's take a simple example of a light not working. It could be the battery, it could be the wiring, it could be the switch, it could be a bad earth at the lamp, it could be the bulb blown or it could be a short circuit.

If the car is starting well and all the rest of the electrics are working you can certainly eliminate the battery for a fault like this, and it's a good plan to look for the simple fault first, in this case the obvious one of a burnt out bulb. The easy way to check this is to use the ohms setting on your meter and test across from the centre contact of the bulb to its body. You should get zero resistance indicating continuity through the bulb filament. If you get no reading at all, in other words infinite resistance, the filament has blown.

Assuming the bulb is all right, the next step is to switch the light on without the bulb in place, set your meter to volts and check between the centre contact in the bulb holder and the outer casing which makes contact with the body of the bulb. You should get close to 12 volts, depending on the state of the battery and the resistance of the wiring or the state of the switch contacts. If you do, the fault is a bad connection between the bulb holder casing and the lamp body. If you get a low reading, or no voltage at all, check between the centre contact for the bulb and a

Quite a lot can go wrong on
ageing headlamps, and you can't
get bits for historic items like
these. Look for water leakage,
rust on the brightwork, and even
missing details

Left Not much space to work in the front compartment of this Ferrari Dino, but removing the spare wheel will help enormously. Several components are mounted close together, which means that there is very little wiring connecting them

Opposite This is the wiring you'd discover behind the dashboard of an MGA if you were agile enough to crawl down into the footwells. It all looks quite simple (and the radio on this particular car is an extra), but be sure you understand the layout before you start to take it all to pieces

Right In the 1940s, before cars got too complicated, you could easily understand dashboard wiring—if, that is, you didn't mind crawling around the floor and ricking your neck to study the problem. If you begin to remove connections, make sure they all well labelled so that you know where to put them back

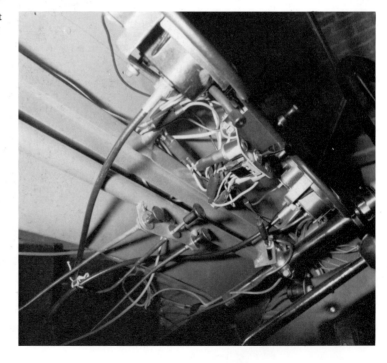

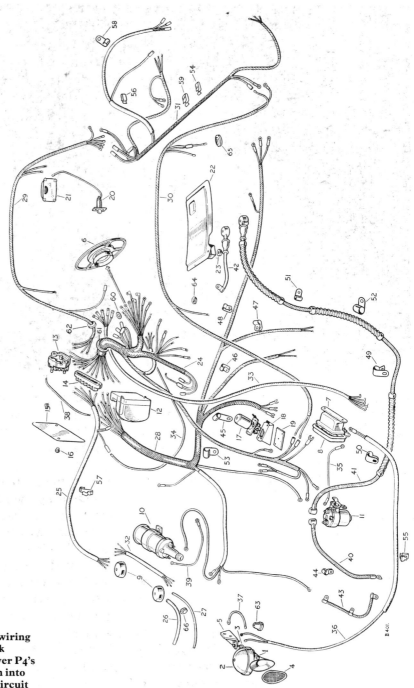

Even by the early 1950s, a wiring loom was beginning to look complex. This was the Rover P4's system, which broke down into several different types of circuit

A useful 'continuity tester' all over the car, is a bulb holder, allied to crocodile clips at each end of the leads. It can save hours

clean part of the body. If this give you a good voltage reading, the fault is a bad earth contact between the body of the lamp and the car body or, if the lamp has a separate earth wire, there is a bad contact somewhere along this. Even if you don't get a good voltage reading here, double check the earth contact of the lamp body by changing your meter to ohms and measuring the resistance between the lamp body and a clean part of chassis earth. Once again you should get almost a zero resistance reading.

Assuming this part of the circuit is all right, but you still get no voltage reading at the centre contact of the bulb holder, look at the wiring diagram to trace the circuit, and check the voltage between chassis earth and the first point in the circuit, usually the fuse box. Check the voltage on the feed to the fuse first, then on the feed from the fuse. If the readings indicate a blown fuse, check the fuse itself either visually, or with the ohms setting, for continuity across it. If it has blown, don't replace it until you have checked to find the cause. It might just be a tired fuse, but it may have behaved in the way it was intended and blown because of a short circuit. A new fuse, and another blow, will confirm it.

Still on the ohms setting of your meter, switch off, leave the fuse out and check between the terminal feeding from the fuse holder, and earth. You should get no reading at all, infinite resistance, but remember that the bulb must be out, or somewhere along the checking you will get a reading through the bulb filament. If there is no contact to earth, replace the fuse and try again.

If you get any indication of contact, the fuse has blown because of a short to earth. Disconnect the cable feeding from the fuse holder and try again at the terminal. If you still get a reading there is a short to earth at the fuse holder. If you get an infinite resistance reading, the short is further along the circuit.

If the fault was not at the fuse holder, reconnect the cable and trace along to the next component, which is probably the switch, and go through the checks again. Somewhere along the line you will find the fault.

Go along the circuit section by section till you find either a break in the circuit or a short to earth. Eventually you will finish back at the lamp again with voltage where it should be.

It has taken a long time to go through this in words, but don't try to remember it parrot fashion. Keep in your mind your two types of basic circuit, feed—switch—component—earth, or feed—component—switch—earth. If it helps, draw out the part of the circuit on which you have trouble, and work out the logical way you are going to check it, first for voltage and then for continuity and for shorts. If you approach it in a logical way, knowing what you are looking for, trouble shooting becomes a detective game with all the odds on your side. You can apply this logical isolating process to almost any circuit on the car, but there are two, the starter and the ignition, where it may be helpful if I go through them in detail.

Any check on the starter circuit should start with a hydrometer test of the battery to make sure it is well charged, and a check on the tightness of the terminals. Follow this

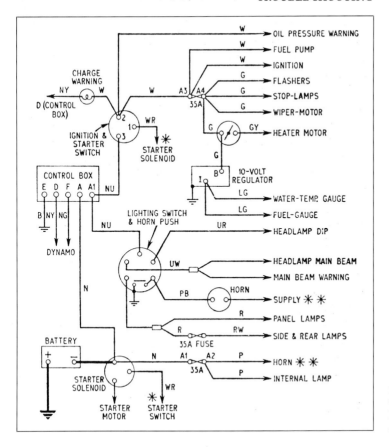

OIL PRESSURE WARNING — W
FUEL PUMP — W
IGNITION — W
FLASHERS — G
STOP-LAMPS — G
WIPER-MOTOR — G
HEATER MOTOR — GY
WATER-TEMP. GAUGE — LG
FUEL-GAUGE — LG
HEADLAMP DIP — UR
HEADLAMP MAIN BEAM — UW
MAIN BEAM WARNING
SUPPLY ✳ ✳ — PB
PANEL LAMPS — R
SIDE & REAR LAMPS — R — RW
HORN ✳ ✳ — P
INTERNAL LAMP — P

Left **The complete but simplified wiring diagram for a 1950s British car—in this case an Austin A40**

Right **A simplified auxiliary wiring circuit, controlled by the ignition switch, and one fuse. The wiring colour is usually green**

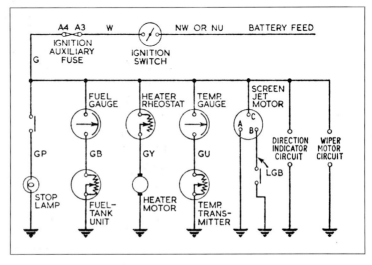

If a battery is old, it may not hold up its voltage under load. Take a low-tension lead off the coil, then connect a voltmeter across the battery while cranking the engine. 10 volts is usual, and 9 volts acceptable, but below this the battery is suspect

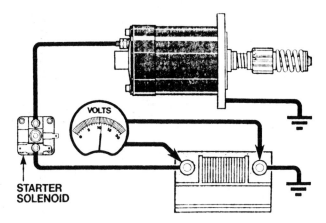

STARTER SOLENOID

The voltage across the starter, under load, should not be more than 0.5 volts below that recorded across the battery. If it is, there is high resistance somewhere along the way

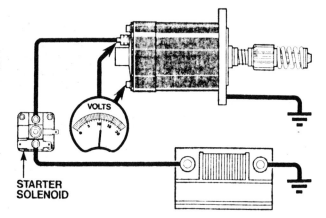

STARTER SOLENOID

This is how to check for high resistance between battery and starter motor. When cranking the engine over, the reading should be nearly zero. If it isn't...

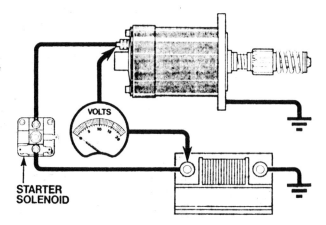

STARTER SOLENOID

... check out the voltage drop across the solenoid terminals. This should be zero, but there may be faults inside the casing

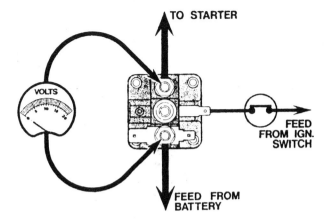

TO STARTER

VOLTS

FEED FROM IGN. SWITCH

FEED FROM BATTERY

As a last check, try the drop between starter body and battery earth terminal, which should be zero. If not, check the connection between the engine/body bonding strap, and the earth connection between battery and body. There could, however, still be trouble inside the starter itself

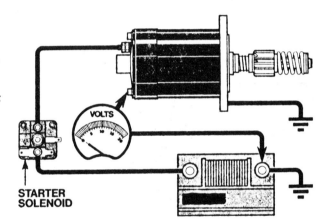

VOLTS

STARTER SOLENOID

by a check on the earth strap from the battery to chassis earth, and the earthing strap for the engine, which usually runs from one of the bell housing bolts. You can test the security by hand, but you need your meter on the ohms setting to check that the bolts are making good electrical contact.

Assuming all is well, check the voltage across the battery *when it is under load* cranking the engine. This should read at least 10 volts from a 12 volt battery. A reading below 9 volts, except on the coldest of mornings, means that the battery is suspect, so take it to a garage for a heavy-discharge test.

Next, move on to check the voltage at the starter motor

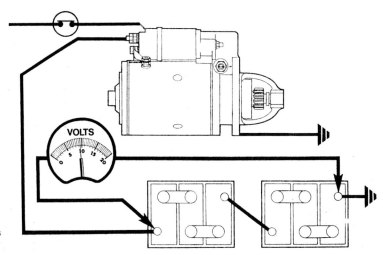

This diagram shows two 6-volt batteries, and a pre-engaged starter, but the check sequence is the same as for an inertia starter

terminals while the battery is under load. It should be no more than 0.5 volts below the reading at the battery. A lower reading means that there is a high resistance somewhere. A little more than 0.5 volts drop might be due to a long cable run from a battery in the boot to the starter, (because all cables have resistance), but if you note much more drop than this, check it out as shown in the diagrams. Check the voltage drop between the live terminal of the battery and the terminal on the starter, then the voltage drop across the main terminals of the solenoid and finally across the body of the starter and the earth terminal of the battery.

With a pre-engaged starter, where the solenoid is mounted integrally with the starter motor, the checks are the same, but remember to use the terminal on the starter itself, except when checking the solenoid, or you might miss a bad connection on the short strap that links the solenoid to the starter. The captions to the diagrams tell you where to find the high resistance.

On the ignition side, the diagrams show two basic circuits, one plain and the other with a ballast resistance in the feed to the coil. On some systems you might find a resistive lead feeding the coil instead of a separate ballast resistor, but the giveaway is the extra lead from the solenoid to the ignition switch side of the coil. The method of check-

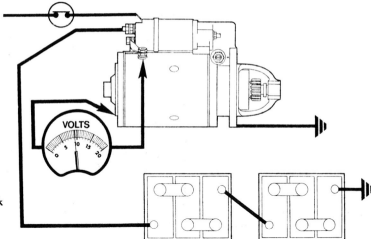

With a pre-engaged starter, check on-load voltage between the starter body, and the starter terminal itself

ing either system is similar, except that you will get different readings on a ballasted system, as the diagrams explain.

Check first that you are getting full voltage to the input side of the low tension circuit of the coil. This will be battery voltage on a plain system, and about half that on a ballasted system. The distributor points are best closed for this check, so that there is current flowing through the coil. If you do not see full voltage, check for a bad connection, or a short to earth in the feed to ignition switch, the feed

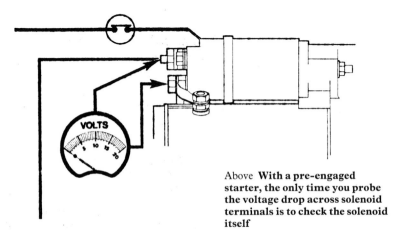

Above **With a pre-engaged starter, the only time you probe the voltage drop across solenoid terminals is to check the solenoid itself**

A typical coil ignition circuit layout, in purely diagrammatic form. The coil in this case is rated at less than 12 volts (9 volts, or even 6 volts is usual), and for normal running the ballast resistor cuts down voltage to suit. For starting, this is bypassed by the feed through the solenoid to the coil

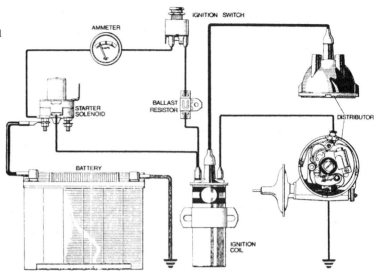

to the coil, or a fault in the ballast resistor.

Now move the voltmeter to the other low tension terminal on the coil, the one feeding the distributor, and turn the engine until the points are open. You should see full battery voltage (or reduced voltage with a ballasted system) when you switch on. If you see a zero voltage reading it means a break somewhere along the line, or inside the coil. Next, disconnect the lead from the coil to the distributor and take an ohms reading between the lead and earth with the points open. If you observe anything but infinite resistance there is a short on the lead or, more likely, inside the distributor, such as the points not opening properly, one of the internal wires shorting, or a cracked or missing fibre washer under the moving point. If you see a full voltage reading with the lead connected to the coil, switch off, take the lead off and check for a perfect contact between the lead and the chassis earth when the points are closed. If you don't confirm perfect contact, check again across the points themselves. You will probably find that they are not making good contact. As a check on the continuity of the coil primary winding, a resistance reading across the terminals should indicate the resistance of the winding. If you see infinite resistance recorded, there is an internal break or burn-out.

Chapter 13 | Rewiring

Rewiring a car is not a particularly difficult thing to do, though it seems somewhat frightening when you look behind the dash and find a jungle of cables. Much of the time on rewiring will be taken up getting at things because when the car was made the wiring looms were far from the last components to be put in.

If you are using a replacement loom from the factory, or one from a specialist loom maker—and there is a surprising number of looms being made for older cars these days—it will be almost the same length as the original. This will not worry a professional auto electrician as he will rip out all the old wiring before he starts, but it makes things very cramped behind the dash if you adopt the procedure I would recommend for the home restorer, which is that of replacing each cable on the car with the identical one in the new loom, one at a time. You can't take the old loom away until all the connections are made.

First of all, you should establish that the colour coding on your loom is exactly the same as that on the car. Check carefully because there are shades of colour which are difficult to distinguish unless you place the two side by side, such as green with a blue tracer and green with a purple tracer. The tracer is the secondary colour of the cable, usually a thin stripe. A surprising number of people have a colour sight problem between similar colours, often without realising it, so if you find you have this difficulty use a few tie-on labels to help with identifications.

The main colour of the cable should be related to the circuit it feeds. There are differences—Ford, for instance, wiring to their own colour code—but the majority of British cars are wired to the Lucas code which uses seven main colours either alone or with tracers to identify different parts of the same main circuit. As a general rule, though there are likely to be exceptions, the live feeds have a single body colour, and feeds from switches to components have the same colour but with an identifying tracer.

For example, plain green is usually used for the feed from the fuse for circuits controlled by the ignition switch, so you could get green cable feeding the stop lamp switch, fuel gauge, heater switch, temperature gauge, direction indicators and wiper switch. Then you could have green with purple tracer from the stop lamp switch to the lamps, green with black from the fuel gauge to the tank unit, green with blue from the temperature gauge to the sender unit, and so on. Earth leads are usually solid black except where components are switched from the earth side (feed-component-switch-earth) in which case the cable from the unit to the switch usually has a black tracer with the main circuit body colour, as for example the cable from the fuel gauge to the tank unit.

The Lucas colour code is usually identified on the wiring diagram by a letter, in most cases the initial letter of the colour, but where colours have the same initial letter, as with B, the standard convention is B for Black, N for brown and U for blue. The colours and their circuits are as follows:

Brown (N), the main colour for the battery feeds to the control box terminals A and B; to the lighting and ignition switches; to the fuse for auxiliaries not controlled by the ignition switch and to the switches of any unfused auxiliaries fed directly from the battery or battery terminal on the control box. Before purple was used, brown with a tracer was also used to feed components from the battery auxiliary fuse, those not controlled by the ignition switch.

Brown is also used as the main colour for cables from the dynamo to terminals D and F on the control box, and between terminal D and the ignition warning light. There is an exception here on older cars, where you might find yellow as the main colour for these cables.

Yellow (Y) was used on older cars as an alternative to brown as above, and on overdrive circuits.

Blue (U) is the main colour for feeds from the lighting

switch to the headlamps.

Red (R) is the main colour for the feeds from the lighting switch to the side, rear, panel and rear number plate lamps and sometimes to the fog and spot lamps, though you may find the spots fed with a blue cable.

Purple (P) is used as the main colour for feeds from the battery auxiliary fuse except on older cars where brown was used.

White (W) is the main colour for feeds from the ignition switch to the ignition auxiliary fuse and to any components controlled by the ignition switch but which are unfused.

Green (G) is the main colour for all feeds to components fed from the ignition auxiliary fuse. Light green (LG) is often used for direction indicator circuits.

Black (B) is the main colour for returns to chassis earth.

It is a daunting list to try to remember, but you will find that as you go along, and study your wiring diagram, the colours begin to stay in your mind. They are a tremendous help when fault finding, as well as when rewiring.

Different people start a rewiring job in different ways, but I would advise starting under the dash. This is most awkward, and once it is done you will feel you have broken the back of the job, if not your neck as well. It is often very cramped under the dash, and to make more room to work once you have established that the colour coding of your new loom is the same as the wiring on the car, saw through the old looms to the dash with a hacksaw and use a knife to strip off the outer woven casing. Then as you replace each cable you can throw the old length out. As you proceed, the job will begin to seem less of a tangle. If there is any secret to rewiring it is to go about it in a methodical manner.

Before you wire in any looms that have to pass through bulkheads, make sure that the loom will pass through the hole once one end of it is connected. Sometimes branches to the loom mean it will pass through the bulkhead in only one direction. Remember to thread the grommet on the loom *before* you pass it through any holes in metal.

Having purchased a loom, you may find that it seems to be incomplete. This sometimes happens where there are bullet connectors in the line as, for example, with headlamps, and the short length of cable from the headlamp to the connectors is part of the lamp and not the loom. It may be stocked separately from the lamp, but under a different part number from the loom. You may also find that there are two, three or even four looms to a car, so make sure you get them all.

If you tackle rewiring without a replacement loom I would advise wiring all in one colour, or at the most two or three, or you will have to buy a large number of lengths of different colour and different tracer cable. In that case, to identify the circuits use slip-on sleeves of plastic on which, if you roughen the surface with glasspaper, you can write the name of the circuit to assist in future fault tracing.

Complete wiring diagrams look so dauntingly complicated, but they can always be split into their component circuits as identified by the main colour of the cable. It pays dividends to sit down for an hour or two to study the diagram before you start, and to sketch out on separate pieces of paper the different circuits. A lot of the complexity disappears when you do this.

Index